Foreign Policy into the 21st Century:
The U.S. Leadership Challenge

Dedicated to
Les Aspin
an exceedingly gifted friend and colleague

Foreign Policy into the 21st Century: The U.S. Leadership Challenge

PROJECT COCHAIRS

Zbigniew Brzezinski
Lee Hamilton
Richard Lugar

PROJECT DIRECTOR AND EDITOR

Douglas Johnston

STEERING COMMITTEE

Carter Beese	Dave McCurdy
Judith Bello	Robert Murray
Harold Brown	Robert Neumann
Richard Burt	Ernest Preeg
William Clark	John Reinhardt
Chester Crocker	Stephen Solarz
Richard Fairbanks	Richard Solomon
Jonathan Howe	Robert Zoellick
Max Kampelman	

September 1996
The Center for Strategic & International Studies   **Washington, D.C.**

About CSIS

The Center for Strategic and International Studies (CSIS), established in 1962, is a private, tax-exempt institution focusing on international public policy issues. Its research is non-partisan and nonproprietary.

CSIS is dedicated to policy analysis and impact. It seeks to inform and shape selected policy decisions in government and the private sector to meet the increasingly complex and difficult global challenges that leaders will confront in the next century. It achieves this mission in three ways: by generating strategic analysis that is anticipatory and interdisciplinary; by convening policymakers and other influential parties to assess key issues; and by building structures for policy action.

CSIS does not take specific public policy positions. Accordingly, all views, positions, and conclusions expressed in this publication should be understood to be solely those of the authors.

Library of Congress Cataloging-in-Publication Data

Foreign policy into the 21st century: the U.S. leadership challenge   /
    editor, Douglas Johnston.
        p.   cm. — (CSIS reports)
      ISBN 0-89206-292-4
      1. United States—Foreign relations—1989 –   2. World politics—1989 –   I. Johnston, Douglas.   II. Series.
E840.F6781996
327.73—dc20   96–34430
                                                              CIP

The Center for Strategic and International Studies
1800 K Street, N.W., Washington, D.C. 20006
Telephone: (202) 887-0200
Fax: (202) 775-3199
E-mail: books@csis.org
Web site: http://www.csis.org/

Contents

Acknowledgments

We move into the twenty-first century much too unfocused as to our nation's role and responsibilities. Our governmental instruments as currently configured appear inadequate to formulating and executing long-term national objectives; our national approach too divisive and partisan. Policymakers have neither the time nor the distance for the kind of studied reflection that is required. Hence the need for an in-depth bipartisan study of this nature that capitalizes on the collective experience and insights of seasoned practitioners and world-class scholars.

Over the past two years, such a group has met under the sponsorship of the Center for Strategic and International Studies and the joint chairmanship of Dr. Zbigniew Brzezinski, Senator Richard Lugar, and Congressman Lee Hamilton. Some 50 experts participating in a personal capacity and on their own time focused on the kind of world the United States should be moving toward and strategized on the best way to get there from here. The discussions were uniformly rich and often inspiring; the debates vigorous and always incisive. This report, which is a consensus document, captures the resulting insights. Its strength lies in the collaborative nature of its development. Throughout their deliberations, the steering committee and seven working groups gave generously of their valuable time and their very considerable talents. The Center and the nation are clearly in their debt.

There are others as well whose efforts have been instrumental in the successful accomplishment of this project. At different times, John Richards, Alexander Nacht, and Dan Magder served as the project coordinator, each doing a superb job of organizing the logistics and providing important substantive input along the way. Special credit is also due Elizabeth Calkins, who typed what must have seemed like several forests worth of drafts, and to Roberta Howard for her herculean efforts in getting the report published in a timely manner. Finally, sincere votes of thanks to Ambassador Robert Neumann for inspiring this effort in the first instance and to the Smith Richardson Foundation for providing the funding support that made it possible.

Douglas Johnston
Executive Vice President, CSIS
September 10, 1996

List of Participants

PROJECT COCHAIRS

Zbigniew Brzezinski	Lee Hamilton	Richard Lugar

STEERING COMMITTEE

Carter Beese	Richard Fairbanks	Robert Neumann
Judith Bello	Jonathan Howe	Ernest Preeg
Harold Brown	Douglas Johnston	John Reinhardt
Richard Burt	Max Kampelman	Stephen Solarz
William Clark	Dave McCurdy	Richard Solomon
Chester Crocker	Robert Murray	Robert Zoellick

WORKING GROUP ON ASIA

Richard Solomon, *chair*	Richard Fairbanks	Gerrit Gong
William Clark	Banning Garrett	Stephen Solarz

WORKING GROUP ON THE UNITED STATES AND EUROPE

Richard Burt, *chair*	Max Kampelman	Anthony Smith
Stanton Burnett	Robert Neumann	Don Snider
Stephen Hadley	Simon Serfaty	John Yochelson

WORKING GROUP ON RUSSIA AND THE NEWLY INDEPENDENT STATES

Robert Zoellick, *chair*	Paula Dobriansky	Thomas Navratil
Keith Bush	James Goldgeier	William Odom
Andrew Carpendale	Walter Laqueur	Brad Roberts

WORKING GROUP ON THE MIDDLE EAST

Richard Fairbanks, *chair*	Joseph Montville	Stephen Solarz
Anthony Cordesman	Robert Neumann	Dov Zakheim
Arnaud de Borchgrave	Peter Rodman	

WORKING GROUP ON INTERNATIONAL SECURITY

Robert Murray, *chair*	Fred Iklé	Brad Roberts
Harold Brown	Edward Luttwak	John Rogers
Arnaud de Borchgrave	Dave McCurdy	Don Snider

WORKING GROUP ON INTERNATIONAL ECONOMICS

Ernest Preeg, *chair*	Penelope	Sidney Weintraub
Carter Beese	Hartland-Thunberg	John Yochelson
Judith Bello	Erik Peterson	

WORKING GROUP ON GLOBAL PROBLEMS AND OPPORTUNITIES

Jonathan Howe, *chair*	Arnaud de Borchgrave	John Reinhardt
Brock Brower	Max Kampelman	Andrew Schmookler
Chester Crocker	Joseph Montville	David Wendt

CONGRESSIONAL SUPPORT

Ken Myers   Michael Van Dusen

PROJECT COORDINATOR

John Richards

Executive Summary

At a time of some confusion in the aftermath of the Cold War, it is important that the United States remain engaged internationally and assert the leadership that most of the world expects and deserves. It is equally important that we have a vision of the kind of world we would like to see materialize and a strategy for moving in that direction. At a minimum, U.S. foreign policy should follow a path consistent with U.S. interests that the American public can understand and support. To the extent possible, this policy should also support our growing interdependence with other nations by advancing globally the basic goals of democratic politics: peace, freedom, justice, order, and the general welfare.

A first order of business for this study was to define and prioritize U.S. interests for the geographical areas of greatest strategic importance to the United States—Asia, Europe, Russia and the Newly Independent States, and the Middle East—and for three functional areas as well: international security, international economics, and a final category labeled "global problems and opportunities." This prioritization is based on whether the defined interests were deemed to be "vital," "important," or merely "beneficial" from a geopolitical point of view.

In general, vital interests are of such consequence that the United States should be prepared to promote them unilaterally by whatever means necessary. Only sometimes will that equate to military action. The one area of this analysis in which the qualifier "vital interest" does not apply is international economics, where the issues are generally not of a geopolitical nature and, in any case, are too interdependent for the distinction of unilateralism to be useful. Although none of the issues addressed in the section on global problems and opportunities currently qualify as vital interests of the United States, left unattended, a number of them are likely to assume that status in the future.

Policy prescriptions are also offered for each of the seven categories cited above. Taken together, these prescriptions aim at a world that is more stable and an international structure that is more democratic and prone toward rule of law. Greater stability is to be achieved through improved economic development strategies, enhanced diplomatic capabilities, and more effective international mechanisms for dealing with international problems (including a United Nations rapid-response capability once that institution's management and procedures have been adequately reformed).

With regard to the international structure, this report recommends that the United States move toward a world in which the number of industrialized democracies is expanded to the point where they constitute a preponderance of the world's economic power, military capability, and population. Not only has history shown that industrialized democracies are among the countries least likely to go to war with one another, but they also have significant trade-related incentives for resolving lesser conflicts in a cooperative manner. Further, and assuming the above structure, they would also have the financial resources to deal more effectively with troubled regions of the world. This recommendation would involve giving higher-priority attention to Latin America, Southeast Asia, and South Asia in addition to Russia and China.

Listed below are abbreviated descriptions of those interests that the steering committee and working groups considered to be the most critical in each of the seven areas covered, along with selected (also abbreviated) policy prescriptions.

☆ ASIA

VITAL INTERESTS

- Preventing domination of the region by an adversarial power.

- Providing security on the Korean peninsula.

- Ensuring commercial, political, and military access to and through the region.

- Containing nuclear weapons and missile technology.

POLICY PRESCRIPTIONS

- Pursue new openings to strengthen U.S. leadership in the Asia-Pacific region.

- Strengthen political and security ties with Japan.

- Work with the People's Republic of China to develop a positive common agenda and a mutually beneficial framework for China's integration into the international economic, political, and security order.

- In concert with South Korea, take steps to increase stability on the Korean peninsula.

- Develop an integrative strategy for South Asia.

☆ EUROPE

VITAL INTERESTS

- Preventing domination of the region by an adversarial power.

POLICY PRESCRIPTIONS

- Continue to play a central role in maintaining European security.

- Propose to our NATO allies that accession talks with Poland, Hungary, and the Czech Republic on NATO membership begin forthwith.

- Take measures to ensure NATO's ability to respond to future crises like Bosnia.

- As feasible, lay the groundwork for negotiating a Transatlantic Free Trade Agreement.

☆ RUSSIA AND THE NEWLY INDEPENDENT STATES

VITAL INTERESTS

- Controlling and reducing Russia's nuclear arsenal.

- Preventing threats to Europe, Asia, and the Persian Gulf in the event of a resurgent and militant Russia.

POLICY PRESCRIPTIONS

- Pursue with renewed commitment the Nunn-Lugar "swords into plowshares" initiative.

- As feasible, purchase additional enriched uranium from Russia and the Newly Independent States (NIS).

- Promote measures to strengthen Russian/NIS nuclear storage and protection policies.

- Prevail on Russia to withhold nuclear technology from states with questionable intentions.

- Continue support for Ukrainian self-help policies.

- Reformulate U.S. aid to Russia for longer-term engagement.

- Seek to address Russian concerns relating to prospective NATO expansion.

☆ THE MIDDLE EAST

VITAL INTERESTS

- Maintaining peace and stability in the Persian Gulf and the availability of oil and gas resources for export.

- Ensuring Israel's survival as a nation state.

- Ensuring the security of Egypt, Saudi Arabia, and Jordan.

- Developing coordinated and more effective responses to Middle East terrorism.

POLICY PRESCRIPTIONS

- Continue support for the Middle East peace process.

- Meet the challenges of Islamic extremism by strengthening moderate governments.

- Encourage aggressive economic reforms and privatization throughout the region.

- Pursue deployment of a theater missile defense capability to protect key U.S. interests in the region.

☆ INTERNATIONAL SECURITY

VITAL INTERESTS

- Protecting the U.S. homeland, including American citizens and property overseas.

- Maintaining unimpeded access to key geographic areas and critical economic resources.

- Ensuring the viability and inclusiveness of the evolving international system.

POLICY PRESCRIPTIONS

- Provide additional foreign assistance to increase the pace and scope of Russian nuclear dismantlement.

- Reformulate foreign assistance to provide more effective support for democratization and longer-term economic development based on free market principles.

- Develop a standing Northeast Asia security dialogue that includes the United States, Japan, China, Russia, and, as appropriate, the two Koreas.

- In Southeast Asia, reinforce the ongoing work of the Association of Southeast Asian Nations (ASEAN) Regional Forum in its broader security deliberations.

- Support and reinforce global treaty regimes for controlling missile technology and weapons of mass destruction.

- Enhance counterproliferation capabilities (especially military).

- Give priority in defense planning to
  - **expeditionary, mobile, deployable forces,** including the deployment of an effective theater missile defense capability, to deter or otherwise cope with external threats to U.S. national interests;
  - **forward military presence** adequate to buttress U.S. diplomacy, build effective security relationships with friendly governments, and deter regional threats;
  - the **strategic nuclear balance** with Russia, including an active national ballistic missile defense research and development (R&D) program to hedge against unexpected developments;

- developing a posture of **incremental readiness** in which the highest levels of readiness are maintained for nuclear-equipped forces, forward-deployed units, and expeditionary naval, air, and ground forces, with lower levels for those components that are expected to deploy later;

- preferential funding of **military R&D** as a way of maintaining technological superiority; and

- increasing the **operational efficiency and cost-effectiveness of the defense establishment.**

☆ INTERNATIONAL ECONOMICS

BASIC "GOALS"

- Sustaining growth of the U.S. economy.

- Sustaining the economic growth of friendly nations.

- Denying the economic well-being of states in which the United States seeks to coerce a change of policy (or government).

POLICY PRESCRIPTIONS

- Strengthen domestic economic performance through strategies that (1) eliminate the budget deficit and encourage higher levels of savings and investment and (2) invest in future generations through effective educational initiatives (both of which are prerequisites to competing in the new economic order).

- Continue to broaden and strengthen the international trade and investment system based on mutual access to markets in the United States and abroad.

- Work to provide a more stable and responsive international financial system.

- Maintain the U.S. leadership role in the international economic system into the next century.

- Provide effective support for a restructured energy sector in Russia and Ukraine that will enable those countries to address the problem of their unsafe nuclear reactors.

- Focus support for the poorest "least developed" countries on project assistance that promotes institution-building and private sector job creation.

☆ GLOBAL PROBLEMS AND OPPORTUNITIES

IMPORTANT INTERESTS

- Combating syndicated and freelance crime, including drug trafficking and terrorism.

- Arresting the downward spiral of development in parts of South Asia, sub-Saharan Africa, and the Caribbean.

- Addressing migration problems.

- Promoting human rights.

- Reversing environmental degradation.

- Eradicating the HIV/AIDS pandemic.

POLICY PRESCRIPTIONS

- Develop an integrated international capability for combating global organized crime, including (at the national level) creation of a Global Organized Crime Committee within the National Security Council and increased information sharing between the law enforcement and intelligence communities.

- Develop a strong U.S. capability in preventive diplomacy.

- Support and selectively strengthen those institutions that can mitigate and resolve disputes, including, among others, the United Nations, the Organization for Security and Cooperation in Europe, the North Atlantic Treaty Organization, the Organization of American States, and the Organization for African Unity.

- Adopt trade and investment policies that facilitate job creation in impoverished countries.

- Sustain, broaden, and intensify U.S. participation in multilateral and bilateral initiatives aimed at environmental protection.

- Support a global response to the HIV/AIDS pandemic.

In summary, as the United States moves toward increasing the number of industrialized democracies, it should focus its energies on two principal objectives: (1) containing the further spread of weapons of mass destruction and the missile technology required to deliver them from afar, and (2) maintaining peace among the major powers.

The costs associated with the above objectives and the other measures prescribed in this report are deemed quite manageable. For the most part, it is a matter of thinking smarter, not richer. But beyond costs, beyond strategy, beyond all else, strong U.S. presidential leadership in international affairs will be the critical prerequisite for the kind of world we would like to pass to future generations, a world where strife is minimized, economic opportunity is maximized, and democratic values hold sway.

Foreign Policy into the 21st Century: The U.S. Leadership Challenge

Steering Committee

Zbigniew Brzezinski, *cochair*
Lee Hamilton, *cochair*
Richard Lugar, *cochair*

Carter Beese
Judith Bello
Harold Brown
Richard Burt
William Clark
Chester Crocker
Richard Fairbanks
Jonathan Howe
Douglas Johnston*

Max Kampelman
Dave McCurdy
Robert Murray
Robert Neumann
Ernest Preeg
John Reinhardt
Stephen Solarz
Richard Solomon
Robert Zoellick

* principal author

1

Foreign Policy into the 21st Century: The U.S. Leadership Challenge

For unto whomsoever much is given,
of him shall much be required.

LUKE 12:48

Tomorrow is ours to shape. More than any time in its past, the United States is strongly positioned to influence the kind of world it would like to see unfold. Globally it is without peer in each of the categories by which one customarily measures international influence: political ideals, cultural resonance, economic strength, and military power. But capitalizing on all this assumes a willingness to do so. As the last presidential and congressional elections seemed to suggest, we as a people have assumed a greater ambivalence toward our international responsibilities. In the aftermath of the Persian Gulf War, for example, we began looking to others to pick up the burdens of global leadership. As the rest of the world recognizes, though, and as the Dayton breakthrough on Bosnia clearly demonstrated, there is no one else.

☆ INTERNATIONAL ENGAGEMENT

U.S. foreign policy since the end of the Cold War has had the appearance of being shaped ad hoc by a myriad of competing and sometimes contradictory objectives. As the United States gropes to find its bearings in the post–Cold War era, one reality remains inescapable: an internationally engaged America is absolutely essential to world stability and security. Yet, in light of limited domestic political and economic stamina for international involvement, exactly what kind of engagement will the country be able to support over the long term? What should our principal objectives be, and what are the best policies and institutions for reaching those objectives?

It seems unlikely that future events will facilitate anything approximating the clarity of Cold War structures, at least not anytime soon. It is nevertheless essential that U.S. foreign policy follow a path consistent with U.S. interests that the American public can both understand and support. The need for consensus, at least on the broader goals, has been made amply clear by the controversy surrounding some of our more recent overseas involvements. Achieving such a consensus, moreover, is made all the more challenging when the standard bearer of one political party occupies the Oval Office and the other party controls both houses of Congress. Even with a Democratic Congress during its first two years in office, the Clinton administration was roundly criticized for its foreign policy failings. Because President Clinton was elected on a domestic platform, international problems largely languished, as in Bosnia, or suffered from missteps, as in the later stages of our Somalian involvement. The two exceptions to this generalization were both economic in nature and last-minute, close calls at that: (1) expansion of the bilateral Canada-U.S. Free Trade Agreement (CUSFTA) to include Mexico, and (2) completion of the Uruguay Round of the General Agreement on Tariffs and Trade (GATT).

More recently, the president's stock has been climbing in the wake of a range of international successes (although a number of them still involve major unresolved issues). Included among these are the fitful progress toward peace in the Middle East; the framework agreement with North Korea that appeared to defuse the immediate possibility of war and that may eventually lead to the elimination of North Korea's nuclear program; the reversal of the military coup in Haiti; extension of the Nuclear Non-Proliferation Treaty and its expansion to include Ukraine, Kazakhstan, and Belarus; U.S. ratification of the START II nuclear arms control treaty; and effective assistance in addressing long-standing conflicts in Mozambique and Angola.

The Bosnia peace accord, which deserves separate mention, is the most recent Clinton success. Here, though, the long-term prospects remain highly uncertain, and the president is faulted for not having weighed in more forcefully at an earlier stage of the conflict. As one British official commented following that accord, "The Bosnia crisis shows that this alliance stands or falls with American leadership. A lot of bickering over the past three years could have been prevented if Washington had taken this kind of assertive approach much earlier."

Bosnia is symptomatic of the kind of problems the United States should be prepared to address more effectively. Regardless of whatever forward planning takes place, however, the choices will always be difficult and domestic political support a challenge to muster. While there is good reason to believe that forceful military intervention in Bosnia at an earlier date might have led to a resolution (of some sort) much sooner, it is important to recall that our allies were opposed to it at the time. And although NATO air strikes clearly contributed to the establishment and success of the Dayton talks, it is difficult to weigh their contribution against the major territorial gains by the Croatian forces leading up to the talks or the cumulative impact of the long-term economic sanctions on Serbia's aspirations.

☆ REASONS FOR INTERVENTION

Following the disappointment of the nation-building aspects of the Somalian intervention, former defense secretary Les Aspin attempted to put that experience in perspective by examining the categories of circumstances being used to justify U.S. military intervention in the post–Cold War era. He defined three such categories: protecting security, protecting interests, and protecting values. The first, which has existed since the founding of the republic, is about protecting the United States, both its people and its territory, from military attack.

Protecting the nation's interests has also been a long-standing requirement, and defining those interests is a principal objective of this report. A recent example of intervening on this basis was our participation in the Gulf War, which was driven by a range of such interests: (1) retaining unimpeded access to the oil reserves, (2) preventing the acquisition of weapons of mass destruction by an unreliable state, and (3) supporting an international system based on the rule of law by punishing the unwarranted invasion of one country by another.

The third category, protecting U.S. values, is more controversial. To be sure, values have long held a place in American history, as evidenced by President Wilson's Fourteen Points, FDR's Four Freedoms, and, more recently, President Carter's vigorous pursuit of human rights. In the context of the East-West confrontation of the Cold War, however, the world often looked to the United Nations and to neutral countries to address a variety of problems relating to values, such as peacekeeping and alleviating starvation. After the collapse of the Soviet Union, though, the world is looking to the United States to play a greater leadership role on these kinds of issues. With the privileges of being the sole superpower come the responsibilities. But often it is more than that. In many cases, the United States possesses the only military capable of doing an adequate job because of its unrivaled lift capacity, command and control, and intelligence capabilities. Thus the United States is looked to for peacemaking in Bosnia, feeding the hungry in Somalia, and supporting democracy in Haiti.

Pursuing such assignments is not without its risks. First, intervening in the internal affairs of other countries, which a "values" agenda often entails, is inherently more complicated than dealing with aggression across borders. Second, there is a danger that using force, or even economic sanctions, to promote values will be seen as a form of cultural imperialism. Third, there is the problem of consistency. On what grounds do we intervene in one civil conflict but not another when neither seems to directly threaten our national interests? Finally, there is less willingness to sacrifice life and treasure to promote values as contrasted with protecting the nation's security and clearly recognized national interests. With limited public support, the exit strategy tends to define the mission, as recent critics have pointed out. And, more often than not, the time frame associated with that mission will be too short to produce an acceptable or stable outcome.

A further and related risk of intervention with limited public support is the prospect of having the rug pulled out if the price gets too high. Eighteen American casualties in a single action in Somalia forced a hasty retreat and the specter of failure, thus overshadowing the significant humanitarian accomplishments of that operation. With further retreats of this kind, would-be opponents will assume that all they need do is inflict a few casualties and their problem will go away.

Complexities aside, values are clearly going to remain a part of the nation's foreign policy agenda. As President Clinton has conveyed in his recent National Security Statements, the United States will send American troops abroad "only when our interests and our values are sufficiently at stake." Moreover, there are times when values are so deeply felt that they can and do elicit strong public support. As the English author G. K. Chesterton is reported to have once expressed it, the United States is a "country with the soul of a church."

☆ COMPETING PARADIGMS

Among the lessons to emerge from recent experience has been the need for more creative thinking about how the United States should relate to and interact with multilateral institutions on security-related issues and, increasingly, on economic issues. The rapid integration of trade, investment, and finance across the world is generating new and unprecedented policy challenges. The world's trading and financial systems are more linked than ever before as new technologies allow capital to flow across borders at the mere stroke of a computer key. At the same time, the dismantling of command economies and "statism" in a number of countries is placing renewed emphasis on market forces and strengthening the influence of Adam Smith's "invisible hand." National economic interests are consequently becoming increasingly linked. This linkage, in turn, either effectively restrains the exercise of national sovereignty over those interests or increases the likelihood that attempts to invoke that sovereignty will damage competitiveness or other national interests.

Thus far, most theses outlining a post–Cold War agenda for the United States have been largely old ideas repackaged. One such thesis champions the continued promotion of free markets and the enlargement of democracy. Another resurrects balance-of-power politics and "spheres of influence." A third advocates collective security anchored by a bolstered United Nations. None of these approaches by itself appears adequate to the full array of challenges that are now emerging.

A lesson of history that we ignore at our peril is that whenever there has been no apparent major threat to our national existence, we as a country have disarmed, turned inward, and let events develop to the point where it required a major war to straighten things out again.

☆ PROJECT GOALS AND FOCUS

If the United States is to walk the line between the polar extremes of isolationism and overcommitment, it will have to lead in shaping a world that is both less chaotic and more amenable to the rule of law. American leadership remains vital to this task, as well as to pursuing its own interests. At the same time, today's array of disparate and often incongruous challenges exceeds the scope of any single country's capabilities or of any simple overarching foreign policy design. For one thing, the breadth and nature of the problems themselves provide no all-encompassing common denominator for analysis or action. Moreover, in the unstructured environment of the post–Cold War world, it will be exceedingly difficult to acquire the public support required to meet those threats that are not perceived as directly challenging U.S. national interests. Witness the intensity of the debate on sending U.S. ground forces to establish and keep the peace in Bosnia.

Accordingly, the first order of business should be to define what those U.S. interests are and to identify our national priorities. A principal goal of this project has been to do precisely that, prioritizing interests on the basis of whether they are "vital," "important," or merely "beneficial" from a geopolitical point of view.

In general, **vital interests** are of such consequence that the United States should be prepared to promote them unilaterally by whatever means necessary. Only sometimes will that equate to military action. The one area of this analysis where this qualifier does not hold true is international economics, where the issues are generally not of a geopolitical nature and, in any case, are too interdependent for the distinction of unilateralism to be useful.

A second goal of this project is to call to the attention of policymakers and the public alike those significant but "nonvital" issues (often global in nature) that, if left unattended today, could become the "vital" problems of tomorrow. Implicit in both goals is the need to make assumptions about the prospective utility and effectiveness of multilateral mechanisms and processes, including some sense of how the cultural disconnects that have plagued our involvement with the United Nations in such places as Somalia and the former Yugoslavia can be addressed.

In conducting this study, four geographical areas of critical importance to the United States have been examined by separate working groups: Asia, Europe, Russia and the Newly Independent States, and the Middle East. These regions were singled out because developments in each are likely to have a major long-term impact on U.S. interests extending well beyond that region's boundaries. Each of the analyses involved assessing current and projected political, economic, and security trends in the region, determining U.S. national interests and goals as they relate to that region, and making clear to policymakers the implications of both.

Comparable analyses have also been conducted of U.S. objectives relating to the functional areas of international security and international economics. Finally, a seventh working group on global problems and opportunities has dealt with cross-cutting issues such as poverty, migration, the environment, and humanitarian assistance, particularly as they pertain to the developing world. It is primarily in the latter two working groups that issues relating to Africa and Latin America have been considered.

The full working group reports are attached and merit careful scrutiny. Each is the result of studied deliberation by a select group of world-class scholars and practitioners. A brief overview of each is provided here as an enticement to your further reading.

☆ ASIA

TRENDS

Looking across the globe over the past decade, one is struck by the contrast between the relative stability and prosperity of East Asia on the one hand and the major problems confronting Europe on the other—problems relating to integration, disintegration, and migration. In Eastern and Central Europe, for example, the Cold War has left in its wake a volatile set of antagonisms that, no longer suppressed, have been finding new expression. By comparison, the generally calmer state of affairs in Asia has been made possible for the most part by (1) the rapprochement between the United States and China over the past 25 years, and (2) the striking political and economic progress attained by Japan, South Korea, Taiwan, and the ASEAN states both individually and collectively. The stabilizing presence of the U.S. Seventh Fleet has also been a factor.

Illustrative of the global economy's inexorable swing toward the Asia-Pacific is the fact that 45 percent of the world's foreign currency reserves currently reside in Asia. Moreover, it is estimated that by the year 2000, 40 percent of all new purchasing power will reside there as well. Developments in the 1990s, however, are calling into question the favorable trends that have facilitated Asia's economic takeoff and the prospect that the twenty-first century will become the Pacific century. Reemergent rivalries and post–Cold War security challenges—some old, some new—are creating uncertainty and anxiety about the future. The mere possibility of a reduced U.S. military presence in the region is already contributing to an arms buildup among the littoral states. The more obvious points of possible friction include (1) the unresolved political and military confrontation on the Korean peninsula, including the imponderables surrounding North Korea's economic crisis, (2) the impact of China's military modernization and the potential for armed confrontation with Taiwan, (3) Russia's uncertain future, (4) economic growth vs. unmet expectations in Thailand, China, and elsewhere, (5) lingering territorial disputes in South and Southeast Asia (particularly India and Pakistan), and (6) overlapping maritime claims in the East China Sea, the South China Sea, the Sea of Japan, and the Gulf of Thailand.

This array of problems only reinforces the considerable sentiment that already exists in East Asia for the United States to continue maintaining regional stability through its military presence, political leadership, and economic engagement. While China and Japan are the major regional powers, each has so far seen its interests best served by the other maintaining stable relations with the United

States. At the same time, each fears the prospect of either collision or collusion between the other and the United States at its own expense.

Like China, Japan is in a state of transition as it adjusts to becoming more of a global player. But as the working group on Asia, under the leadership of Ambassador Richard Solomon, suggests in appendix A, the nature and extent of Japan's future role will relate in significant measure to the sense of threat it feels from China. For the near term, the success of President Clinton's Spring 1996 "security summit" in Tokyo suggests that Japan is likely to remain content "leading from behind" in East Asia, securing its commercial and security interests through a continued reliance on U.S. strategic leadership.

INTERESTS

As is the case in other parts of the world, preventing any adversarial power from dominating the region is a vital interest of the United States.   The working group notes that the chief challenges in this regard are (1) effectively integrating an increasingly powerful and assertive China into the international order in a way that is consonant with U.S., regional, and Chinese interests; and (2) successfully managing our complex and vital relationship with Japan as that country seeks to redefine its role consistent with its economic and political power.

A second vital interest is maintaining security on the Korean Peninsula based on our alliance relationship with South Korea, as North Korea deals with its economic crisis and political uncertainties.   One aspect of this challenging situation is North Korea's undiminished and highly threatening conventional military posture, which must be reduced if there is to be a relaxation of tensions on the peninsula and if North Korea is to cope adequately with its economic decline.

Another vital U.S. interest is ensuring continued commercial, political, and military access to and through the region.   A related consideration is the need for the United States to ameliorate the tensions between its allies in Seoul and Tokyo stemming from the legacies of the colonial era and World War II. Above all, however, no power or combination of powers should be permitted to delink the region from North America through exclusionary security or economic groupings or policies.

Finally, there is the all-encompassing vital interest of containing the proliferation of weapons of mass destruction, primarily nuclear weapons and missile technology, but also biological and chemical weapons and related agents. Beyond the proliferation threats posed by China and North Korea, there are the parallel concerns of Pakistan's intentions and the recent successful test firing by India of its new Prithvi-II missile. Despite recent peaceful overtures between India and Pakistan, the potential for their ongoing tensions over Kashmir to escalate to the point of nuclear warfare is a continuing concern that must be taken seriously by all states in the region. India's recent refusal to agree to terms for a comprehensive test ban treaty only underlines the difficulty.

Among those interests that one might label as "important" are the peaceful resolution of competing offshore territorial claims in the South China Sea; observance of human rights norms; and regional cooperation through multilateral forums, e.g., the Association of Southeast Asian Nations (ASEAN) and the ASEAN Regional Forum (ARF); the Asia Pacific Economic Cooperation initiative (APEC); the South Asian Association for Regional Cooperation (SAARC); and the Council for Security Cooperation in the Asia Pacific (CSCAP), a "track II" nongovernmental body.

POLICY PRESCRIPTIONS

Based on the above interests and other considerations, a number of policy prescriptions are offered:

- **Pursue new openings to strengthen U.S. leadership in the Asia-Pacific region.** The resurgent competitiveness of American industry coupled with the ongoing desire of many Asian countries to counterbalance other commercial powers (especially Japan) and anchor America's long-term commitment to the region could provide a unique opportunity for even more effective economic involvement than in the past.

- **Strengthen political and security ties with Japan.**   In the recent past, the United States was the subject of two parallel concerns on the part of the Japanese: (1) "Japan bashing," in which continued pressure from Washington on the U.S. trade and current account deficits reaped political resentment in return, and (2) "Japan passing," in which U.S. policy was seen as bypassing Japan in an effort to appeal to China. Both of these concerns have faded, however, as issues of security have recently supplanted those relating to trade and as the deterioration in Sino-American relations has rendered moot any perception of "passing." Japan is now principally concerned that U.S. mismanagement of its relations with China could draw Japan into a Sino-U.S. confrontation.

- **Work with China to develop a positive common agenda and a mutually beneficial framework for Chinese integration into the international economic, political, and security order.**   At the same time, encourage China to recognize international norms in the area of human rights and quietly indicate U.S. determination to resist efforts by China or any other country to impose solutions on the territorial disputes in the East and South China Seas by force of arms (or threats to use arms).

- **Reconfirm U.S. determination to see a peaceful evolution of relations between China and Taiwan.**   In the course of reaffirming to both parties the U.S. commitment to a "one China" policy, make it clear that the United States will resist provocative acts by either side to alter the status quo in the Taiwan Strait. Continued implementation of this policy will require unusually deft diplomacy in light of (1) U.S. commitments to China as conveyed in the three Sino-American communiqués, (2) our own domestic legal requirements associated with the Taiwan

Relations Act, and (3) the changing domestic political circumstances in China and Taiwan.

- **In close collaboration with South Korea, take steps to increase stability on the Korean peninsula** as North Korea contends with its deepening economic and political crisis. To the extent possible, these steps should include stabilization and reduction of the military confrontation to the point of a mutual pullback of forward deployments in the area of the demilitarized zone (DMZ) and a reduction in North Korea's defense spending—now estimated at more than 20 percent of gross domestic product (GDP)—in the context of new security arrangements for the peninsula.

- **Develop an integrative strategy toward South Asia.** Through a combination of promoting economic development in the region, cooperating in UN peacekeeping operations, and increasing military-to-military contacts, the United States should seek to gain added leverage for enticing India and Pakistan to sign both the Nuclear Non-Proliferation Treaty (NPT) and the Comprehensive Test Ban Treaty (CTBT) and for curtailing nuclear and missile competition on the subcontinent. In addition, the United States should support the efforts of the South Asian Association for Regional Cooperation (SAARC) and promote increased links between SAARC and other regional organizations such as ASEAN and APEC as a means for addressing long-standing regional disputes (and for more effectively integrating South Asia into the international political and economic arenas).

Left unmentioned in the above listings of interests and policy prescriptions is what might be catalogued as a **beneficial interest, i.e., supporting initiatives to maintain the ecological health of the region.** Environmental problems loom large in Asia, particularly in China. As the working group points out in appendix A, Beijing has openly stated that it will not sacrifice economic growth for the sake of the environment. Already that country is experiencing water shortages in most of its cities as a result of industrial waste dumpage and has lost croplands equal to all of the farms in France, Germany, Denmark, and the Netherlands combined. And yet, for Beijing to feed its people, it must either find a way to double its grain output over the next 20 years or be prepared to make massive purchases in the international markets. Asia's ecological problems in the coming century are likely to prove severe, if not overwhelming, to the states in the region and will most certainly pose a special challenge to U.S. leadership.

☆ EUROPE

TRENDS

The recent return of France to the command structure of NATO as part of the Bosnia peace initiative has been an encouraging development. More generally, though, the years since the end of the Cold War have been marked by a degree of discord between erstwhile European allies and accompanying tendencies toward disengagement. The factors contributing to these unsettling developments are explored at some length in appendix B by the working group on Europe under the leadership of Ambassador Richard Burt and Dr. Simon Serfaty. In capsule form, "As the fear of old enemies recedes, the appeal of old friends fades."

Perhaps nothing has demonstrated the resulting weakness so dramatically as the Bosnia peace accord. It was only after intensive U.S. engagement that the situation finally took a turn for the better. Foremost among the factors that contributed to European ineffectiveness was the unfortunate sequencing in which "peacekeeping" and humanitarian assistance preceded the essential tasks of "peacemaking." The latter simply cannot be pursued effectively in a context in which "peacekeepers" are subject to being held hostage. But beyond the inability of Britain, France, and Germany to agree on a common course of action, the ability of Europeans to mount a major military campaign on their own is greatly hindered by inadequate intelligence capabilities, airlift, and other forms of logistics support.

Neither the United States nor Europe can afford to go their separate ways. Europe is simply too critical for the United States to write off politically, economically, or militarily. Conversely, left to itself, Europe is too weak to balance Russian power or sustain German security.

INTERESTS

Preventing domination of the region by any adversarial power has been and will remain a vital U.S. interest.   Part and parcel of this is the need for an effective transatlantic security framework that not only keeps the United States directly involved in European defense but provides a capability for addressing collectively the many problems of instability that currently plague Eastern and Central Europe and the former Soviet Union, of which the former Yugoslavia is but one example. Preserving NATO as the institution most directly responsible for Europe's security and for the security of U.S. interests in Europe (and other areas of mutual concern, such as the Persian Gulf) is of crucial importance.

Heading the list of important U.S. interests in Europe are the challenges of change. Foremost among these is the need to extend the "common European space" to other states that belong to similar traditions and that are seeking membership now that the Cold War is over. Beyond enlarging NATO as a way of strengthening democracy and reassuring the independence of the former Warsaw Pact states of Eastern and Central Europe, the European Union (EU) should also be enlarged to include the more eligible applicants. Just as U.S. policies during the Cold War gave the states of Western Europe the boost they needed to launch the European Community and later the EU, it is now their turn to provide a similar boost to their eastern neighbors who long for economic prosperity and solid security ties to the West.

Another important interest is to achieve a deeper sense of unity between the United States and the EU and among EU members.   Until Europe reaches a final agreement on what the architecture of unity should look like, U.S. interactions with Europe will continue to have significant bilateral dimensions, depending on whether the issues are transatlantic or intra-European. A new structure of EU-American relations needs to be defined.

Finally, there is the need to nurture an environment in Europe that is economically dynamic and politically stable.   For the foreseeable future, Europe's status as a major and reliable trading partner will continue to be a critical ingredient in America's economic well-being. Thus the United States should continue to preserve and strengthen the common political, economic, and cultural bonds created in Europe and across the Atlantic during the Cold War.

POLICY PRESCRIPTIONS

With these vital and important interests in mind, the following policy prescriptions are recommended:

- **Continue to play a central role in maintaining European security.**

- **Propose to our NATO allies that accession talks with Poland, Hungary, and the Czech Republic on the question of NATO membership begin forthwith.** Although actual membership should be tied to implementation of the necessary military and civilian reforms required to perform as a reliable ally and related to each country's ascendancy to the EU before the end of the century, a commitment to begin the process at this time will give added hope to the reformist elements within these countries. Enlargement itself will help stabilize Europe by consolidating an expanded zone of democracy and by anchoring Germany in a broader strategic, political, and economic framework.

Among the points of concern that have arisen in this debate is that relating to cost. Although estimates vary widely, the assumptions that yield combined defense-related expenditures of approximately $35 billion over the next 10 years (to be shared by the United States, the United Kingdom, France, Germany, and the candidate states themselves) are thought to be the most credible. Assuming this cost figure or something close to it, the U.S. portion is unlikely to impose an excessive financial burden.

It is in the U.S. interest that accession talks on NATO enlargement no longer be deferred. At the same time, NATO should reassure those other candidate states in the region not yet ready for full membership of its continued commitment to their independence—perhaps through periodic joint military exercises and enhanced cooperation under the Partnership for Peace program. It should also take steps to reassure Russia through comprehensive security, economic, and political cooperation.

- **Take measures to ensure NATO's ability to respond to future crises like Bosnia.**   The June 1996 agreement of the NATO foreign ministers to give European nations greater independence in launching military operations without active

U.S. participation (under the combined joint task force concept) is a good first step in this direction. Broadening the focus of future NATO operations beyond the original East-West parameters will be yet another. These measures and others still to be conceived will enhance NATO's flexibility and increase its future effectiveness.

To quote the working group report in relation to Bosnia, "Despite NATO's late but decisive insertion of force under strong and decisive U.S. leadership, no one can forget the sense of outrage and shame felt at the sight of the atrocities that could have been avoided before they started, should have been ended before they escalated, and will now have to be prevented lest they resume." Another failure to respond to such a challenge elsewhere in Europe could call NATO's future existence into serious question. If we and our allies do not uphold those parts of the UN charter and the Helsinki Final Act that oppose aggression, the principle of nonaggression will become irrelevant.

- **Develop a strengthened transatlantic coordination process for addressing out-of-area, out-of-Europe issues.** Specifically, the European Union should include U.S. participation in all of its institutional settings just as the U.S. government should upgrade its relations with the EU at all levels, e.g., the European Commission and its various directorates, the Council of Ministers, the European Parliament, and the European Court of Justice.

- **Examine the feasibility of negotiating a Transatlantic Free Trade Agreement,** with an eye toward possible implementation on the 50th anniversary of the signing of the Rome Treaties that established the European Economic Community (March 2007). U.S. domestic political support may present a challenge, but such an initiative is made all the more important by existing moves toward free trade agreements across the Pacific and in the Western Hemisphere.

For most of its existence, NATO has suffered from a chronic case of political "disarray" in one form or another. "Whither NATO?" has been the enduring question. Yet in the face of crisis, NATO has proven to be one of the most effective, longstanding alliances in history. Its considerable strengths have more than offset its acknowledged weaknesses, and they will continue to do so once the necessary post–Cold War adjustments are completed. Member states that used to wage war with one another on a more or less regular basis have not done so for 50 years now. Twice in this century an American absence in Europe led to world wars, ultimately at great cost to the United States in lives and treasure. The stakes are simply too high to risk a repeat. To avoid it, we will need to overcome recently expressed isolationist tendencies and acknowledge that our destiny is linked inextricably with that of Europe.

☆ RUSSIA AND THE NEWLY INDEPENDENT STATES

TRENDS

Taken together, the challenges confronting Russia and the Newly Independent States (NIS) border on the overwhelming: converting to a market economy from one historically based on strict price controls and centralized economic planning; establishing democratic societies where they have not previously existed; and developing "normal" as opposed to hierarchical relationships between Russians and the non-Russian segments of the former Soviet empire. Any one of these challenges would represent a tall order in and of itself. That these countries are dealing not only with a collapse of empire and severe economic distress, but a failed ideology as well (and all that this suggests in terms of social readjustment), compounds the difficulties.

As the Russia/NIS working group under the leadership of former under secretary of state Robert Zoellick suggests in appendix C, there are three plausible scenarios relating to future developments in Russia: (1) muddling through the reform process, eventually developing a relatively stable democracy and market economy, (2) continued weakening of the state and society in which neither the reformers nor their opponents prove capable of forging a new system, and (3) a general resurgence of authoritarianism, either individual or bureaucratic, in response to the frustrations of the first scenario or the fears of the second.

Despite the differences of these widely varying scenarios, the near-term implications for Russia's external policies are essentially the same for each. Russia's primary security objective will be to preserve the territory of the Russian Federation—no small task considering the ethnic tensions and secessionist tendencies that have already arisen and that are unlikely to disappear anytime soon.

Of almost equal importance in Russia's security calculus is the stability and pro-Russian orientation of the other states of the former Soviet Union, or, as they are collectively labeled, the "Near Abroad." This concern underlies Russia's current emphasis on developing and strengthening the institutions of the Commonwealth of Independent States (CIS), particularly as they relate to the integration of military capabilities, air defenses, and border controls. In this context, the geographic range of Russian interests varies from the Caucasus, which are seen as providing a strategic buffer against Iran and Turkey (and militant Islam), to the Caspian Sea with its immense natural resources, to the Baltics with their important "window on the sea." In each of these areas, protecting the rights of the "Russian minorities" offers a convenient rationale for intervening militarily if political cost is deemed commensurate with probable gain.

Lagging far behind the above objectives for the Russians is that of maintaining cooperative relations with the West. Although the effectiveness of Western assistance has always been dependent on Russian self-help, the romanticized expectations of major Western aid have since fallen prey to disillusion; and now many Russians think the West has not only misled them, but is seeking to weaken them through deliberate manipulation.

INTERESTS

With these Russian interests in mind, the corresponding vital interests of the United States include first and foremost the reduction and secure control (by

Russia) of Russia's nuclear arsenal. After the major arms control agreements that have already been negotiated are fully implemented and the full effect of ongoing dismantlement programs is felt, it is estimated that the Russians will still have about 3,500 strategic and 8,000 nonstrategic nuclear warheads distributed throughout the country (or at sea). And herein lies a real dilemma: with these weapons left intact, the command and control capability of a disintegrating empire creates a level of concern that did not exist even when the numbers of weapons were considerably higher. Dismantled, on the other hand, the component parts, especially the weapons-grade fuel, can become vulnerable to acquisition by terrorist groups and renegade states if not disassembled and stored under very tight controls.

A second vital interest is to avert (or limit) the threat that a future resurgent and militant Russia would pose to Europe, Asia, or stability in the Gulf. As Zoellick notes, "Russia is the only country that could potentially threaten our partners across both the Atlantic and Pacific."

Underlying each of the above concerns is a more general uncertainty relating to the actual size of the problem. When Kazakhstan asked the United States to remove and store its highly enriched uranium, the U.S. government recovered 104 percent of its declared inventory. As Senator Lugar pointed out at the time, "Consider the implications of a 4 percent error margin in the Russian inventory."

Heading the category of important U.S. interests relating to Russia and the NIS is a successful reform program in Russia leading to democracy and a free market system. Another important U.S. interest is the continuation of peaceful relations between Russia and Ukraine. As Zbigniew Brzezinski has long championed, a free and independent Ukraine is not only fundamental to the future of European stability, it is the sine qua non in avoiding renewed Russian imperialism. Critical to Ukraine's success as an independent state is an effective economic and political reform program.

Additional important interests include stable relations between Russia and China, the continued independence of the Baltic states, and Russian respect for the sovereignty of the remaining Newly Independent States.

At the level of a beneficial interest is Russian cooperation with Western policies in the United Nations and elsewhere.

POLICY PRESCRIPTIONS

The following policy guidance is offered:

- **Pursue a course of realistic engagement with Russia.** Whether Russia becomes democratic or reverts to authoritarianism, we should pursue our interests in cooperation with the Russian Federation to the extent that proves possible. While we should reach out to Russia wherever we can, we should also hedge against the possibility that future relations could sour, combining firmness with conciliation.

- On the nuclear front, (a) pursue with renewed commitment the Nunn-Lugar "swords into plowshares" initiative, (b) to the maximum extent feasible, purchase additional enriched uranium from Russia and the NIS, (c) promote measures to strengthen Russian/ NIS nuclear storage and protection policies, and (d) prevail on Russia to withhold nuclear technology from states with questionable intentions, such as Iran.

- Continue support for Ukrainian self-help policies both bilaterally and through international financial institutions.

- Reformulate U.S. aid to Russia for longer-term engagement, looking to the multilateral institutions for general economic support while targeting small bilateral grants at specific helpful initiatives such as institutionalizing a free press. An added component is the task of opening Western doors to Russian trade.

- Offer to address Russian concerns relating to prospective NATO expansion through creative mechanisms such as a NATO-Russia treaty or charter that recognizes and, to the extent appropriate, accommodates Russia's interests and the specificity of its concerns, and/or alternative consultative arrangements perhaps involving a subset of the Organization for Security and Cooperation in Europe (OSCE), with rotational leadership.

Because of the immense domestic hurdles Russia is traversing, there is an understandable tendency among Western policymakers to discount Russian concerns in other policy areas. Russia, while weakened, remains a formidable military power and is unlikely to forget slights, however unintended. At the same time, it is important that we remain assertive in pursuing (1) our own interests, particularly those relating to nuclear proliferation, (2) our need to develop theater and (as needed) national missile defenses, and (3) the continued independence of the nations of Central and Eastern Europe and the Newly Independent States.

☆ THE MIDDLE EAST

TRENDS

Despite the intermittent progress toward peace between Israel and its Arab neighbors in recent years, the Middle East will remain an area of concern well into the next century. Iraq, with its provocative behavior and the strongest land forces in the Gulf, continues to command attention on an all-too-frequent basis, and the long-term intentions of Iran and Syria with their ongoing sponsorship of terrorism and buildups of high-tech weaponry remain highly suspect. In addition, the generic specter of radical Islam (as contrasted with the many more moderate elements of Islam) looms large on an overarching basis, fed specifically by the active support of Iran but more generally by the failure of secular governments to meet the minimal expectations of their populations. The World Bank ranks the economic performance of the Middle East and North Africa over the last decade as the worst of any region in the world. Rapid population growth coupled with declining per capita income and a breakdown of urban infrastructures and educational systems are taking a heavy toll on the ability of governments to govern.

As the Middle East working group under the leadership of Ambassador Richard Fairbanks notes in appendix D, the region's general failure to adopt comprehensive economic reforms has been a major contributor to existing social problems. Intense militarization has also been a factor, although less so today than in the past. Measured in constant 1994 dollars, military expenditures have fallen from $97.2 billion in 1991 to $45.1 billion in 1994 and currently account for 6.4 percent of all imports to the region. Despite this favorable trend, Russia's increasingly assertive Middle East policy, especially its cooperation with Iran, could provide renewed impetus to the problem of militarization (although Russia should be every bit as concerned as the West, if not more so, about Islamic extremism and nuclear proliferation, especially in its neighboring areas).

In addition to the reduction in military expenditures, there are other positive developments that should be noted. First, the Arab-Israeli peace process, until recent interruptions, has already led to greater economic cooperation, particularly between Israel and Jordan (and some of the Gulf states). Second, U.S. political and military influence in the region has increased greatly as a result of the Soviet collapse and the later coalition victory in the Gulf War. Third, key nations such as Egypt, Israel, Morocco, and Tunisia have now begun a process of internal reform, although the pace and depth of that reform understandably varies according to each country's unique circumstances. Barring a total breakdown in the peace process, these events have effectively tipped the traditional balance of power in the favor of Arab moderates with which the United States has close ties (particularly Egypt, Jordan, and Saudi Arabia) at the expense of the more radical states. Strategic cooperation and an enhanced U.S. military presence, including strong power projection capabilities, have contributed significantly to improved regional stability (despite the occasional forays of Saddam Hussein and the debilitating effects of ongoing terrorist activity). This increased influence is also translating to stronger economic development through increased privatization and reduced barriers to foreign investment.

INTERESTS

The United States has four vital interests in the region: (1) ensuring peace and stability in the Gulf and the availability of oil and gas resources for export, (2) continuing our special relationship with Israel, with the concurrent obligation to ensure Israel's survival as a nation state, (3) supporting the governments of Egypt, Saudi Arabia, and Jordan against threats to their security, and 4) developing a coordinated and more effective response to Middle East terrorism.

Important interests include (1) Arab-Israeli peace, (2) stable energy prices unencumbered by regional disruption or political/economic blackmail, (3) security for other Arab partners in the Gulf, (4) stability in the Maghreb and North

Africa, (5) closer ties between Turkey and the West, and (6) promoting political liberalization to encourage the rule of law and human rights as norms in those Middle Eastern states where currently they are not.

A key **beneficial interest** is the imperative to demonstrate to Arab populations—particularly those segments at the bottom rungs of the economic ladder—that capitalism and market mechanisms can directly improve their lives.

POLICY PRESCRIPTIONS

At the policy level it is recommended that the United States

- **Continue its support for the Middle East peace process**, providing such security guarantees as may prove necessary and feasible. Prime Minister Binyamin Netanyahu's victory in Israel's June 1996 elections has clearly altered the tactical situation and shaken perceptions, but it does not change basic American interests. Nor does it change the U.S. commitment to a just, stable, and lasting peace based on the principles of UN Resolutions 242 and 338. Terrorists simply cannot be permitted to wield a veto over the peace process.

- **Continue to contain Iran militarily while encouraging it to change its policies.** More specifically, if Iran agrees to end its support of terrorism, its violent opposition to the Arab-Israeli peace process, its efforts to obtain weapons of mass destruction, and the more threatening aspects of its military buildup, the United States, in turn, should be more forthcoming in its political and economic relations, e.g., by relaxing its opposition to loans and trade with Iran and by facilitating Iran's access to international organizations and lending institutions.

- **Continue to contain Iraq militarily.**

- **Meet the challenges of radical Islam by strengthening moderate governments**, such as those of Egypt, Jordan, and Saudi Arabia, and by developing additional diplomatic and economic options for dealing with the causes of instability in the region.

- **Encourage aggressive economic reforms and privatization throughout the region**, without which neither the peace process nor positive political evolution will ever fully succeed.

- **Reevaluate the practice of specifying precise amounts of foreign assistance for selected states and prohibiting changes to accommodate changed circumstances.** Aid can be a powerful and cost-effective tool for advancing U.S. strategic interests in the Middle East, and marginal increments to selected countries can produce disproportionately beneficial results.

- **Encourage regional dialogue, joint study, and negotiations on limiting missiles and weapons of mass destruction in the region.** At the same time, pursue deployment of a theater missile defense capability as an urgent strategic priority to protect key U.S. interests in the region.

- **Develop long-term cooperative security arrangements** based on (a) existing bilateral security agreements with key allies in the region; (b) informal arrangements with the Gulf Cooperation Council; (c) contingency planning with European allies, particularly Britain and France; and (d) out-of-area planning within NATO.

The Middle East will continue to be a difficult and Delphic part of the world, with no single touchstone for sweeping positive change. Strategically, the United States should continue its current long-term approach, but with the added emphases noted above. In sum, we must support movements toward peace, counter the proliferation of weapons of mass destruction, and confront military aggression directed against those states in which we have a vital interest.

☆ INTERNATIONAL SECURITY

TRENDS

With the disappearance of the only hostile counterweight to U.S. military power, the United States virtually stands alone in its ability to wield influence across the international stage. Indeed, U.S. military strength is so dominant that it will be a decade or two before any other nation-state could be in a position to pose a credible challenge to our global influence.

Complementing this security framework are the economic changes that are moving nations toward market economies and liberal democracy. Because these changes are creating a greater number of stakeholders in the international system, a corresponding incentive is created for resolving peacefully those differences that arise within the system.

On the other hand, there are powerful nations like Russia and China that have yet to fully buy into this system, as well as less powerful states like Cuba, North Korea, Iran, Iraq, and Libya, which for varying reasons are disinclined toward international cooperation. Finally, there are the non-state actors, such as terrorist groups and the multiple factions of global organized crime that actively pursue destabilizing agendas. Collectively these states and groups constitute a formidable challenge to international security and will require an ongoing posture of vigilance, a capacity for preemption, and a ready response on the part of the system's stakeholders.

INTERESTS

America's security interests are many and varied. As emphasized in appendix E by the International Security working group (first under the leadership of the late former defense secretary Les Aspin and later under Robert Murray, former director of national security programs at Harvard), **foremost among our vital interests is the age-old requirement of preventing direct threats to the homeland.** With the increasing proliferation of technology, long-range missiles, and weapons of mass destruction, this concern will only grow over time. There is also the ongoing vulnerability to international terrorism, whether in the form of violent attacks against population and infrastructure or in the form of cyberterrorism directed against communications, defense installations, and banking systems through the various computer networks on which they depend. By extension, "homeland" is also meant to include American citizens and property overseas.

A second vital interest is ensuring that hostile powers do not dominate key geographic areas or critical economic resources. In this regard, preserving the stabilizing presence of NATO becomes a critical factor, as does maintaining intact our bilateral security relationship with Japan. This interest constitutes *the* driving factor in determining the size and capabilities of U.S. military forces.

Finally, the United States has a vital interest in maintaining the viability of the evolving international system and ensuring that it is as inclusive as possible. The welfare of the United States and most other countries depends on continued U.S. leadership in the existing international network of economic, political, diplomatic, and security relationships and institutions.

The working group has classified four other national interests as important to our security: (1) promoting and enhancing regional stability; (2) promoting the economic and political development of underdeveloped, troubled nations; (3) advancing human rights; and (4) advancing the common security interests of friendly states in bilateral and multilateral association, including support for the role of the UN in regional peacekeeping and peace-enforcing operations.

At the level of **beneficial** interests, the working group believes that **encouraging closer military-to-military relationships and other forms of nation-state cooperation** will facilitate achieving the objectives cited above and strengthen the basis for conducting coalition operations should the need arise.

POLICY PRESCRIPTIONS

The following policy prescriptions are recommended:

- **As feasible, provide additional foreign assistance directed toward increasing the scope and pace of Russian nuclear dismantlement.** This is seen as a singularly cost-effective security investment.

- **Reformulate existing foreign assistance in such a way as to support more effectively the processes of democratization and longer-term economic development based on free-market principles.**

- **Strengthen security in Europe through cooperative arrangements between Russia and an expanded NATO.**

- **Work in partnership with Japan to bring China into the international community, and with both to maintain peace in Asia.**

- **Develop a standing Northeast Asia security dialogue** that includes the United States, Japan, China, Russia, and, as appropriate, the two Koreas. In Southeast Asia, reinforce the ongoing work of the ASEAN Regional Forum in its broader security deliberations.

- **Support and reinforce global treaty regimes for controlling missile technology and weapons of mass destruction.**

- **Improve counterproliferation capabilities** (especially military).

- **Task the Departments of State and Defense with jointly developing and maintaining a "lessons learned" library** of past intervention experiences, government-wide contingency planning for future interventions, and a program of education and training on these subjects for cabinet officials and department/agency staff.

- **Place a greater emphasis on issues of peacemaking and peacekeeping in the education and training curricula of military schools and war colleges.**

- **Give priority in defense planning to**
  1. **expeditionary, mobile, deployable forces**, including the deployment of an effective theater missile defense capability to deter or otherwise cope with external threats to U.S. national interests;
  2. **forward military presence** adequate to buttress American diplomacy, build effective security relationships with friendly governments, and deter regional threats;
  3. **the strategic nuclear balance with Russia**, including an active ballistic missile defense R&D program to hedge against unexpected developments;
  4. **developing a posture of incremental readiness** in which the highest levels of readiness are maintained for nuclear-equipped forces, forward-deployed units, and expeditionary naval, air, and ground forces, with lower levels for those components that are expected to deploy later;
  5. **preferentially high levels of military R&D** as a hedge against the possibility of other countries gaining technological superiority over the United States; and
  6. **increasing the operational efficiency and cost-effectiveness of the defense establishment.**

None of these policy prescriptions, however, will be as important to the security interests of the United States as the continued willingness of the president and the Congress (and, by extension, the American public) to take leadership on security matters within a posture of international engagement.

☆ INTERNATIONAL ECONOMICS

TRENDS

The decade of the 1980s brought with it a sea change in U.S. international interests on two fronts. First, the fall of the Berlin wall led to a regionalization of security problems and a corresponding reduction in their importance; and, second, unprecedented technological innovation produced a wide-ranging impact on the global economic system and led to an ascendancy of political/economic issues in national decision-making.

This impact on the global economic system has been characterized by (1) more open (i.e., trade-dependent) national economies; (2) a broadening of international transactions beyond trade in goods to trade in services, international investment, and technology transfer; (3) increased globalization of financial markets; (4) a tri-polarization of international trade and investment in which the course of the world economy, including the growth effects of new technology applications, is dominated by North America, Western Europe, and East Asia; and (5) a strengthening of the earlier multilateral system based on nondiscrimination and (through the GATT Uruguay Round agreement) its expansion to include comprehensive regional free trade agreements and selective bilateral accords.

An interdependent global marketplace has become a new reality requiring a new policy focus. Economic interests are heavily interrelated and, as such, can be addressed only in a comprehensive fashion that integrates considerations of international trade, investment, and finance with domestic economic policies. As pointed out in appendix F by the International Economics working group under the leadership of Ambassador Ernest Preeg, "national sovereignty is progressively constrained as a practical matter by a deepening network of economic policy commitments, trade dependencies, and large volumes of private capital flows." Not only are governments constrained in the extent to which they can oversee and regulate economic activity within their territories, but the surge in private flows has diminished the influence of international financial institutions like the International Monetary Fund (IMF) and the multilateral development banks (MDBs).

INTERESTS

U.S. economic interests can be stated briefly in terms of three basic goals:
(1) **sustained economic growth of the U.S. economy** (to provide improved economic well-being for the American public and the necessary resources for pursuing other national interests); (2) **sustained economic growth in other friendly nations** (to provide reliable markets for U.S. goods, to help ensure a more stable and cooperative international order, and to provide an enhanced capability for multilateral funding of mutually desired objectives); and (3) **the denial of economic well-being in those states where we seek to coerce a change of policy** (or even government).

Maintenance of an open-market international economic system is the overarching interest that should drive most other aspects of U.S. economic policy. Toward this end, the multilateral, regional, and bilateral tracks should be managed in a mutually reinforcing way that leads to balanced market access, more effective rules, and more equitable dispute procedures for the trade and investment system.

For the international financial system, the goals should be to promote capital formation and reduce unnecessary regulatory barriers while encouraging greater transparency of data.

POLICY PRESCRIPTIONS

To achieve these ends the following short- to medium-term policy objectives are offered according to whether they are "vital," "important," or "beneficial" to U.S. interests (note: this use of these terms differs from how they are used in the other working group papers, where the distinction refers to the geopolitical significance of a particular interest).

Vital:

- **Strengthen domestic economic performance** through strategies that (1) eliminate the budget deficit and encourage higher levels of savings and investment and (2) invest in future generations through effective educational initiatives (both of which are prerequisites for competing in the new economic order).

- **Continue to broaden and strengthen the international trade and investment system** based on mutual access to markets in the United States and abroad.

  1. implement the Uruguay Round agreement, including the early incorporation of financial and basic telecommunication services in the World Trade Organization (WTO), and bring investment and related competition policies under the WTO umbrella at such time as this proves possible;

  2. pursue as a next goal of trade liberalization a major extension of zero-for-zero tariff elimination by sector to eliminate tariffs on most nonagricultural trade;

  3. develop improved procedures for dealing with trade-related environmental issues and possibly, after further study, labor standards as well;

  4. extend comprehensive regional free trade agreements to include other geographical areas and structure them so that they create rather than divert trade (as building blocks toward more open trade on a multilateral basis):
     a. extend NAFTA to include Chile and other countries in the Western Hemisphere;
     b. support full membership in the EU of Poland, Hungary, the Czech Republic, and other countries that may qualify;
     c. lay the groundwork for a transatlantic free trade initiative that builds on the Clinton administration's Transatlantic Agenda; and
     d. explore the feasibility of an open-ended OECD (Organization for Economic Cooperation and Development) free trade agreement that would encompass the EU, NAFTA, and the more advanced East Asian countries;

  5. pursue bilateral trade objectives in policy areas not covered by the multilateral system such as investment and competition (a top-priority bilateral

objective with China, for example, is effective protection of intellectual property rights).

- **Actively encourage a more stable and responsive international financial system:**

    1. strengthen the IMF's role in monitoring and ensuring transparency of national economic policies and providing emergency financial assistance;

    2. encourage cross-border regulatory cooperation to ensure a coordinated response capability in times of financial crisis; and

    3. take policy actions to lower regulatory costs in private capital markets, harmonize standards in capital markets (to reduce "friction costs" across borders), and support capital market infrastructure in developing countries.

- **Maintain the long-standing leadership role of the United States in the international financial and economic systems into the next century.** Thereafter, the continued diffusion of economic power will require that it be increasingly shared with the EU, Japan, and the next tier of industrialized countries. As an important prerequisite, educate the American public on the importance of U.S. international economic interests.

Important:

- **Restructure foreign assistance programs** to more effectively support U.S. objectives pertaining to democratization and longer-term economic development.

- **Link support for transitional former Soviet bloc countries to the implementation of economic reforms** relating to privatization, market-based pricing, fiscal balance, and trade liberalization. Target such assistance toward specific bottlenecks in the reform process and channel it as much as possible through the private sector.

- **In concert with Europe, provide effective support for a restructured energy sector in Russia and Ukraine** that will enable these countries to address the problem of their unsafe nuclear reactors.

- **Focus support for the poorest "least developed" countries on project assistance to support institution-building and the creation of private-sector jobs** in order to fortify civil society and the center of the political spectrum against destabilizing threats from the right and left. To the extent possible, channel this aid through the private sector and nongovernmental organizations (NGOs).

The emerging global economic system may have far more profound implications for international politics than are first apparent. As mentioned, economic interdependence is already having an impact on national sovereignty as governments find it increasingly difficult to cope with the more than $3 trillion of private capital that flows across national boundaries each day. Of even deeper political significance, though, is the degree to which economic liberalism and liberal democracy reinforce one another.

With the above in mind, **the working group has posited as a long-term objective a paradigm shift for the international economic system in which the number of industrialized democracies is expanded to the point where they constitute a preponderance of world economic power, military capability, and population.** Two important causal linkages support such an approach: (1) the well-established correlation between market-oriented liberal trade policies and faster economic growth (and hence a basis for broader industrialization and modernization) and (2) the growth of decentralization and democratic tendencies as a national economy reaches the more advanced stages of industrialization.

The rationale for effecting such a shift is threefold. First, history has shown that industrialized democracies are among the countries least likely to go to war with one another. Second, those countries would also have significant trade-related incentives to resolve lesser conflicts in a cooperative manner. Finally, they would have the financial resources to deal more effectively with the troubled regions of the world.

If one accepts that such a shift is desirable, it then becomes a matter of moving toward that new paradigm over the next several decades while guarding against the year-to-year possibility of a breakdown in the existing political-security order (as smuggling and unemployed Russian scientists exacerbate the spread of weapons of mass destruction, and numerous ethnic tensions threaten global stability through their spillover consequences).

This dual requirement suggests a need to reorder U.S. foreign policy objectives to give Latin America, Southeast Asia, and South Asia greater attention (along with China and Russia). As the working group points out, the challenge to U.S. global strategy is to forge an amalgam of the new economic and security realities so as to "create a more prosperous, stable, and truly new world order."

☆ GLOBAL PROBLEMS AND OPPORTUNITIES

TRENDS

In the wake of the great bipolar confrontation, the world's most pressing problems and, in some respects, its greatest opportunities can be found in the developing countries. The impulse toward socialism and central planning that dominated so much of the nonaligned movement has all but totally disappeared—at least on the surface—and left in its place a changed attitude toward the United States, which is now widely admired for its economic competitiveness and political success. Further, reduced great power rivalries have created a window of opportunity for addressing the root causes of a number of major world problems that heretofore have largely been finessed, such as wide-scale poverty and disease, environmental degradation, organized crime, and the more general breakdown of society in certain parts of the world. Symptomatic of the scope of these problems is the related problem of overpopulation and the challenges it poses for the carrying capacity of the planet.

The United Nations projects that, by the year 2025, world population will have increased from today's 5.7 billion people to between 7.6 and 9.4 billion. This equates to adding a population the size of Mexico's every year or the size of China's every decade. Thus far, increases in agricultural productivity have averted a Malthusian collapse. They may continue to do so, especially if harvesting food supplies from the ocean depths becomes a reality. Since 1945, however, 11 percent of the world's arable land has been degraded—an area equal to the size of China and India combined—and per capita food production is now declining in many developing countries. Population displacements, which are greatly affected by this, currently stand at 50 million, including international refugees and those who have been internally uprooted.

Ironically, at the very time that much of the world hungers for American leadership and support in addressing these and other global problems, there has been a significant move toward retrenchment on the part of a number of American politicians and opinion leaders. This tendency has been driven by an understandable desire to relax our international vigil in order to address a range of pressing domestic problems. But the leadership vacuum that would result from such an abdication is likely to create much larger problems downstream, problems to which the United States will not be immune. While these problems currently qualify as "important" or "beneficial" U.S. interests, left unattended a number of them will eventually escalate to the "vital" category.

As the most influential and pace-setting member of today's emerging global society, the United States is uniquely positioned to lead through engaging others in identifying common problems and devising coordinated solutions. In so doing, it would be wise to build upon what has gone before by adapting existing structures to meet future challenges wherever possible. As the working group on Global Problems and Opportunities under the leadership of Admiral Jonathan Howe states in appendix G, "There is nothing to be gained through a policy of systematically starving these institutions and programs of resources, denigrating their accomplishments, diluting and watering down their structures, circumventing their mechanisms and procedures. . . ."

INTERESTS

The United States should prioritize its approach to global problems by focusing first on those that represent the greatest threats to its near- and long-term interests and to its values. After building the necessary public support, it should then marshal its resources, in coordination with those of other countries, wherever international action has the greatest chance of producing a favorable outcome.

High on any list of important U.S. interests is combating the spread of syndicated and free-lance crime. The increased lawlessness that is threatening the physical security and quality of life of U.S. citizens as well as others around the world is largely a result of global criminal networks that are well-organized, coordinated, flexible, and far more efficient than most national law enforcement organizations. The international drug cartels are particularly menacing in this regard. Through their ongoing shipments of cocaine, heroin, and other narcotics, they contribute directly to the countless acts of crime that plague the world on a daily basis.

If law enforcement is unable to confront and dismantle these rapidly growing international networks, then the entire political structure of some nations will be at risk. For example, organized crime is one of the principal threats to Russia's chances of emerging from economic distress and consolidating a foundation for new democratic institutions—a key strategic issue for the West.

Internationally coordinated terrorist groups are of even greater concern. The bombing of the New York World Trade Center and the chemical attacks on the Tokyo subway illustrate the vulnerability of civilian infrastructure to such attacks and raise the fearsome specter of terrorism linked to weapons of mass destruction.

Arresting the downward spiral of development that is occurring in parts of South Asia, sub-Saharan Africa, and the Caribbean is also an important U.S. interest.   In these places, poverty, population growth, and environmental degradation have been compounding one another to produce a situation in which GDP has been lagging behind population growth over the past decade and a half. As the working group notes, "These places may be strategic backwaters, but the longer the world's wealthy 'suburbs' ignore its deteriorating 'slums,' the more the slum dwellers themselves will be tempted to look for other neighborhoods"—which raises the related problem of cross-border population movements fueled by economic disparities and large-scale civil disorders.

Although the United States has thus far been spared from the burdens of mass migration that are beginning to weigh heavily on Europe and China (internally), addressing problems of dislocation at their source is an important U.S. interest. The mere specter of this kind of problem helped inspire our most recent intervention in Haiti and our earlier initiative to extend the bilateral U.S.-Canadian free trade agreement to include Mexico (with which the United States shares one of the world's longest borders between any industrialized and developing country). Despite the extensive moat off both its coasts, the United States is also clearly vulnerable to the problem of human smuggling, especially from the south. In short, there is no immunity from this problem.

One of the many contributors to the pressures for migration (and other sources of political instability) that deserves separate mention is the global HIV/AIDS pandemic, which has already devastated much of sub-Saharan Africa and which recent projections suggest may infect more than 100 million people by the turn of the century. For this and other disease epidemics, the United States should support a global response through UNAIDS (the newly established coordinating body of the United Nations) and through nongovernmental and private volunteer organizations. Such matters should be given the higher-priority concern they deserve and be treated as serious security, economic, and social problems.

Echoing the international security assessment, **advancing human rights is also deemed an important interest.** As noted by steering committee member Ambassador Max Kampelman, there has been a discernible shift in the dividing line between "internal affairs"—those not to be interfered with by other states or by the UN—and the need to hold states responsible for adhering to the human rights they undertook to enforce when they signed the UN charter and other international agreements.

Simultaneous with the development of greater intrusiveness by the United Nations and increasingly conscious of its duty to preserve peace and vital human values, the OSCE (then CSCE) extended its own license in this regard through broadening and extending the 1975 Helsinki Final Act. By 1991, all signatories, including the Soviet Union, had agreed that "issues concerning national minorities . . . and commitments concerning the rights of persons . . . are matters of legitimate international concern and consequently do not constitute exclusively an internal affair of the respective state."

That said, the working group felt there should be limits to what the United States does in this regard and flexibility in how it goes about it. In an era of increasing interdependence, it was felt that a uniformly aggressive public pursuit of our human rights agenda would not always be effective and might, in some cases, prove counterproductive to the total range of U.S. interests. However, there are some universal values—accepted even by those who preach a difference between Western and Asian values—for which we should hold firm in our support, even if we need to assert them less publicly.

Finally, **reversing the problems of environmental degradation is an important interest for all nations**, whether or not it is uniformly recognized. Quality of life is directly at stake when dealing with most issues of this nature, e.g., nuclear disposal, oil pollution, ocean dumping, over-fishing, large-scale soil erosion from the illegal harvesting of trees, acid rain, ozone depletion, and global warming.

While debate continues on many of these problems, there is an increasing institutionalization of environmental rules and guidelines embedded in international agreements, national environmental policies, and business practices. Translating this evolving policy framework into action, however, remains a major challenge. Few countries have been willing to incur substantial costs or to forgo economic growth to limit environmental damage. International environmental cooperation is constrained by the wide variation between countries in pollution per capita, total population, economic growth, energy use, and natural resource endowments.

Humanitarian intervention, which in terms of its geopolitical implications for the United States should properly be categorized a beneficial interest, often assumes a greater importance from the standpoint of U.S. leadership in world affairs.   Reconciling national interests with humanitarian traditions will always be difficult, as has been recently demonstrated in Somalia and Bosnia where our national interests were difficult to define but where we ultimately found it impossible not to act. So long as the fighting in the former Yugoslavia was confined to the immediate region, the conflict had little to do with any direct U.S. national interest (other than that of preventing its spread). But watching an unfolding genocide over time without doing anything to stop it would eventually undermine our sense of national morality. At such times as we do intervene, however, we should do so with our eyes open as to our key objectives and provide the necessary resources to achieve them. (Ideally, such interventions should be undertaken on a multilateral basis). As has been widely recognized, the fact that we failed to match resources to objectives in Somalia caused most critics to label that effort a failure, even though countless Somalis were saved (some estimates run as high as 300,000) from death by starvation and disease. **Without equivocation, the United States should seek to prevent genocide when and where it can be prevented.**

POLICY PRESCRIPTIONS

Among the policies the United States should pursue (jointly with others) in response to the above interests are the following:

- **Develop an integrated international capability for combating terrorism and global organized crime.**   The free world can no longer afford to cede the high ground of tight coordination, advanced technology, and modern weaponry to criminal elements. As an important first step at the national level, two recommendations of the Commission on the Roles and Capabilities of the United States Intelligence Community are particularly relevant: (1) creation of a Global Organized Crime Committee of the National Security Council to be chaired by the National Security Adviser and to minimally include the Secretaries of State and Defense, the Attorney General, and the Director of Central Intelligence, and (2) increased information sharing between the law enforcement and intelligence communities, including the collection by intelligence agencies of information about non-U.S. citizens outside the United States when so requested by U.S. law enforcement agencies (as used in the Commission's report, the term "Global Organized Crime" subsumes terrorism). Both of these recommendations can and should be enacted by presidential executive order.

- **To the extent feasible, adopt trade and investment policies that facilitate job creation in impoverished countries.**   Expanding NAFTA to include other countries of South America, for example, will minimize the stream of economic refugees seeking jobs here. Either countries will export their goods or they will export their people. With nearly half of the world's population under the age of 20 and a sizeable share of them at or below the poverty line, the need for jobs will grow even more severe in the absence of proactive policies.

- **To minimize the social costs of economic restructuring, gauge the pressure we apply on other countries in pressing for political and economic reform.**   As the working group notes, too much too soon can backfire and create bigger problems than existed in the first place.

- **In continuing to press for human rights around the world, remain engaged with those countries whose policies in this area may be inconsistent with our own but where it is otherwise in our interests to do so.** As the working group notes, our preferred role is to create openings for improved conditions through persuasive dialogue and engagement.

- **Sustain, broaden, and intensify participation in multilateral and bilateral initiatives aimed at environmental protection.** In particular, explore and exploit "win-win" approaches through market-based incentives and increased flows of capital and environmental technology to developing countries.

- **Develop a strong capability in preventive diplomacy.** Although the costs of maintaining an effective preventive diplomacy capability pale in comparison to the costs of forcible entry once conflict has erupted, there is strong movement in the U.S. Congress to cut back heavily on what limited capability already exists in the State Department and other organizations. Because a preventive approach requires a great deal of patience (the results are not always guaranteed or even apparent when they are realized) and discipline (paying now to avoid paying more later), exploiting its full potential will require a concerted appeal to the American public in credible cost-benefit terms they can both understand and support. Here again, though, priorities are important. A strategy of preventive diplomacy that seeks to prevent everything is likely to end up preventing nothing.

- **Support confidence and security building measures (CSBMs) to the extent they do not undermine U.S. national interests.** CSBMs exist in many parts of the world and should be viewed as integral to any effective preventive diplomacy capability. Designed to promote a transparency of intentions between nation states, they include a wide array of approaches ranging from communications hot lines to joint military exercises to nuclear free zones to agreements specifying procedures to be used in provocative situations, such as the Incidents at Sea Agreement between Russia and the United States. CSBMs take many other forms as well, most of them useful to promoting peace.

- To hedge against the inevitable conflicts that preventive diplomacy will be unable to forestall, the United States should **support and selectively strengthen those institutions that can mitigate and resolve disputes, including, among others, the United Nations, the OSCE, NATO, the Organization of American States (OAS), and the Organization of African Unity (OAU).** Efforts to build vibrant economies and durable democracies are doomed to failure when undertaken in a context of basic internal and regional insecurity. In Africa, for example, too many of that continent's important states (Zaire, Algeria, Sudan, Liberia, Nigeria, Angola) are either in the midst of conflict or perilously close to it. The United States should give a high priority to resolving and managing conflict in Africa through bilateral diplomacy, greater allied coordination and support for strengthening Africa's regional security institutions, selective and targeted support for African peacekeeping operations, and active partnership with NGOs engaged in the region.

The concept of a volunteer, trained, and ready UN rapid response force is an idea whose time may be coming, even though several major problems would have to be overcome for such a concept to become a reality. Foremost among them is basic reform of the UN's management structure and procedures in order to eliminate waste, provide sharper accountability across the board, and establish confidence in the UN's ability to manage a rapid reaction capability. After that, there are the specific challenges to be addressed relating to infrastructure funding, command relationships, and the availability and training of troops. Once established, such a force would provide an important option for policymakers as they seek to respond more effectively to shared world interests. If organized and executed properly, such a capability could help avoid the conflicting calculations of national interest that currently plague UN operations.

Regional peacekeeping organizations, however, should constitute the first line of defense in addressing many of these problems and, as such, should command our full support. The United States has, in fact, been assisting in the fuller development of peacekeeping capabilities in such organizations as the OAU. Offering even greater potential cohesiveness in this regard are selected subregional organizations like the Southern African Development Community (SADC). This same logic holds true for other regions as well. In today's strife-torn world, it is difficult to imagine having too much of such capabilities.

- **Promote the internationalization of curriculums in colleges and other academic institutions**, with a particular emphasis on issues of global interdependence, language skills, and the understanding of foreign cultures.

The financial costs associated with the above prescriptions (as well as the other measures recommended in this report) are deemed to be quite manageable. For the most part, it is a matter of thinking smarter, not richer. The real bottom line to meeting these seemingly intractable global problems, however, is U.S. leadership—no easy commodity without the domestic constituency to support it. But building constituency is a critical component of exerting leadership in a democracy, and that is the task to which we turn next.

☆ SYNTHESIS: THE GRAND DESIGN

The basic question that inspired this project in the first instance was what can the United States actively do to shape a better world. Implicit in this question is the ability to define what that better world would look like. Here, two conditions come to mind: greater stability and an international structure that is based on democratic principles, free-market mechanisms, and the rule of law. Assuming continued U.S. primacy in defense capabilities, the first goal of reducing conflict will be best served through improved diplomatic capabilities and better mechanisms for dealing with international problems.

INCREASED REQUIREMENTS FOR DIPLOMACY

Before hostilities broke out in the former Yugoslavia, the president of Yugoslavia sent a message to the U.S. Sixth Fleet Commander requesting increased visits to Yugoslav ports as a way of showing the flag and helping to keep things under control. The State Department recommended against it, and the request was denied. The reasons for doing so undoubtedly seemed compelling at the time, i.e., that the United States had no desire to get involved in Yugoslavia, that it was a European problem, and that it was more properly a matter for diplomacy. Whether such visits could have made a difference will never be known, but this is the kind of activity that is properly associated with the rubric of preventive diplomacy, a capability the United States needs to develop in much greater measure (witness the ambiguity of our diplomatic signals to Saddam Hussein prior to the Gulf War).

In an increasingly untidy world in which Americans are reluctant to support military intervention, the U.S. Congress should be allocating additional resources to the tools of diplomacy rather than cutting them back. Diplomacy backed by capability and resolve is designed to prevent the need for military force; and the diplomat is as vital a part of our national security as the soldier, sailor, or airman. Further, diplomacy has now become a critical component in advancing our national economic interests in an increasingly competitive global marketplace. Moves to weaken our diplomatic assets are thus clearly out of sync with a world that is growing strongly interdependent. But it is not simply a matter of retaining or enhancing the traditional tools of diplomacy. It is about developing improved instruments for active intervention in evolving situations before they become problems and developing better mechanisms for resolving conflict once problems do develop. It is also about building on the historic strengths of the nation-state model of international relations by capitalizing more effectively on the contributions of NGOs and, in some instances, private citizens.

IMPROVED INTERNATIONAL MECHANISMS

Accepting the reality of our commitment to certain values, we as a nation need to face up to the challenges this commitment presents and confront the difficult choices that need to be made. On the one hand, we are deeply disturbed by the endless string of global atrocities that parade across our television screens—but not so much that we are inclined to intervene unilaterally. On the other hand, we are unwilling to develop a true international combat intervention capability under UN auspices either because we consider the UN to be ineffective or mismanaged or because we are unwilling, as a matter of principle, to place U.S. forces under UN command. Further, we are customarily delinquent in paying our normal dues, including our share of the costs for UN peacekeeping operations. In short, it becomes a "Catch 22." But as Ambassador to the UN Madeleine Albright stated several years ago, "Whether measured in arms proliferation, refugees on our shores, the destabilization of allies, or loss of exports, jobs, or investments, the cost of runaway regional conflicts comes home to America . . . without the UN, both the costs and the conflict would be far greater."

To be sure, the United Nations needs to mend its ways (as detailed in appendix G), but it also needs the proper tools to do the job one should rightfully expect of it. Most U.S. policymakers discount the concept of a UN rapid response force on the grounds that the command and logistics problems are too intractable or because they believe that the American public would never support it. Among other indicators, they point to the paranoia of extremist groups against government in general and the UN in particular. Yet a recent polling of Americans by the Wirthlin Group (December 1995) showed "overwhelming support for creation in the U.S. armed forces of a special contingent of volunteers that would be available for UN peacekeeping assignments, and the conviction that U.S. participation in the UN will be 'very important' in coming years—even more important than membership in NATO." Commenting on the poll, John Whitehead, former deputy secretary of state and now chairman of the UN Association-USA, observed: "When you compare the latest data with those of prior years, what is most striking is the consistent growth in the American people's preference for handling international problems through international institutions. There seems to be no constituency at all for the alternative of unilateral action." So there may be more room to maneuver than many might think.

The oft-cited problems of command and control, funding, and logistics, while formidable, are solvable and should be given priority attention. Here, the "Vanguard Concept" described in the September 1995 report of the Canadian government entitled *Towards a Rapid Reaction Capability for the United Nations* should be given serious consideration. This concept entails a multifunctional force composed of up to 5,000 military and civilian personnel from nationally raised units of volunteers. These units, which would be earmarked and trained for UN duty, would be made available under enhanced standby arrangements (which the UN Secretariat would conclude with those member states willing to provide personnel for peace operations). Of course, individual governments would continue to have the final say on whether their units could be used—an important proviso because political resolve will always be *the* critical factor in determining the effectiveness of any multilateral approach to peacemaking. But having the kind of capability outlined above and the planning and organizational structure to support it could make it easier politically for member states to join forces when timely intervention would make a major difference. As the UN commander in Rwanda stated, "A force of 5,000 personnel rapidly deployed could have prevented the massacres in the south and west of the country that did not commence in earnest until . . . nearly a month after the start of the war."

The financial and political costs of establishing and maintaining such a standby capability should be weighed against those of continuing on the current ad hoc reactive basis, with all that goes with it, i.e., ill-defined missions, inadequate forces, divided leadership, inordinate command delays, and the loss of face that accompanies failure. As for the problem of who is to command such a force, if the United States is deemed indispensable to the operation, then it should be in command. Short of that, command should perhaps be exercised by that country having capable military leadership that contributes most to the effort in terms of funding and manpower.

In addition to developing an enhanced UN capability, equal priority should be given to supporting regional peacekeeping and conflict resolution capabilities, as the United States has been attempting to do in Africa through the OAU and in Europe through the OSCE. In addition to providing an improved frontline capacity for indigenous problem-solving, these organizations also offer a backstop for those situations in which the UN may be unable to act because of a veto or insufficient votes in the Security Council.

TOWARD A NEW STRUCTURE

Returning to the earlier-discussed need for a structural shift in the international economics paradigm, it is strongly recommended that the full implications of such a move be analyzed and an effective strategy for moving in this direction be developed as a matter of national priority. Such a strategy should include renewed U.S. leadership for strengthening and broadening the trading system at the multilateral and regional levels (as outlined in appendix F), a judicious retargeting of our political dialogue, and more effective development assistance provided in concert with other developed countries.

On this latter note, two financial assistance tools that the United States has been using with some success in Central Europe and elsewhere and that deserve special consideration for future application are (1) enterprise funds, in which government money is channeled directly to the private sector through investment corporations formed by private U.S. citizens and the host country where the fund is to be located, and (2) privately managed venture capital funds supported by investment guarantees of the Overseas Private Investment Corporation (OPIC). Both vehicles are designed to be self-sustaining and to encourage development of the host country's economy through U.S. capital and expertise.

In the meanwhile (near- to mid-term), we should give our highest priority to the two problems in which the United States has the most directly at stake. The first is preventing the spread of weapons of mass destruction and the missile technology required to deliver them from afar. New measures should be developed for all three levels of interaction: prevention, deterrence, and engagement. Of particular urgency on all three fronts is the long-overdue need to create a streamlined and more accountable U.S. government structure for addressing the full range of proliferation-related issues. Special attention should also be given to the previously mentioned but largely overlooked issue of tactical nuclear weapons, of which the Russians are currently estimated to have more than 8,000 distributed at 150 different sites.

The second problem is that of maintaining peace among the major powers. Although touched on tangentially in some of the working group reports, this challenge deserves further amplification. Consistent with human nature, when things are going well in a relationship (or when there are no immediate causes for concern), there is a tendency to take the other for granted and to overlook the need for preventing things from going wrong. At the moment, U.S. policymakers appear increasingly sensitive to the implications of our interactions with China, largely as a result of the growing prominence that country will assume in the future.

We should also maintain our guard with respect to Russian sensitivities. In at least two major (and justifiable) ways, we are testing the resiliency of our relationship with Russia in our efforts to guard against possible future attempts to reestablish its former empire. First, we are directly buttressing Ukraine as a free and independent state and are fully supporting the independence of the Baltic States. Second, and what Russians see as more provocative, we are preparing to expand NATO to the east. The recent rise to power of communists in a number of Central and East European states and in Russia's parliamentary elections may give added cause for concern and perhaps a greater sense of urgency in moving ahead (although the "new" communists, at least in Central Europe, appear more reform-minded than their predecessors, and Yeltsin's recent reelection provides added reassurance further to the east). Still, it is critically important that the United States do all it can to work with Russia in promoting comprehensive security arrangements between Russia and the West.

Beyond the ongoing need to hedge against Russia's capability to destroy the United States, if not the entire planet, that country also deserves close attention as a factor in managing whatever world order emerges. **As has already been seen on more than one occasion, partnership with Russia represents the strongest possible hand for dealing with international uncertainty.**

At the same time, we should take great care not to provide incentives for China and Russia to cooperate at America's expense. As a possible counterweight to unexpected developments in either of these two countries, the United States should nourish a close relationship with India. At current rates of population growth, India's population will overtake that of China early in the next century (its middle class alone already outnumbers the total population of the United States). Despite its many internal difficulties and past strains in our bilateral relationship, India is democratic, has a formidable military, and is achieving impressive economic gains under the stimulus of economic reforms. In short, India could represent a helpful force in facing an uncertain future.

LEADERSHIP REVISITED

The single theme recurrent in all of the working group reports is the need for strong and assertive U.S. leadership in international affairs (for our own interests as well as the world's more generally). As such, the subject merits a much fuller discussion and is the final topic of this report. There are at least three reasons why this theme receives so much attention. First, the international landscape has changed dramatically and represents an entirely new set of challenges. As was the case in the wake of total victory following World War II, policymakers are feeling their way through a period of significant uncertainty and confusion and are understandably criticized for the tentative and seemingly ad hoc nature of their decision-making. This translates in the eyes of many abroad as well as in the United States to a "leadership problem."

Second, and compounding the above difficulty, are certain ingrained institutional problems relating to the functioning of government. In the Congress there is the ongoing tension between efficient decision-making and unfettered individualism, exacerbated in recent years by the breakdown of the seniority system. At the other end of the power axis, depending on who occupies the Oval Office, the ebb and flow of power between the executive and the Congress that was exacerbated by the Watergate experience has confused both the public and other governments and introduced added uncertainty into the decision-making calculus of most policymakers.

As much as we as a country might feel tempted to turn inward, we simply have too much at stake in other parts of the world to do so. In recognition of this reality, steps should be taken to achieve greater bipartisanship in our foreign policy. A useful first step would be for whatever administration is in power to institutionalize a process of tighter coordination with the bipartisan leadership in the Congress on major foreign policy themes. Further, as a matter of routine, members of the opposing party should be included in ad hoc presidential commissions and certain oversight bodies relating to foreign policy, such as the President's Foreign Intelligence Advisory Board and the Board for International Broadcasting.

Exacerbating the institutional difficulties is a major lack of public trust in the institutions themselves. As reflected in a recent national survey, only one in four Americans trust the federal government all or most of the time. This contrasts with three out of four who exhibited such trust three decades ago.

Third are the generic obstacles to effective leadership that are growing only more intense with time. Beyond a general awareness of their existence, they are for the most part assumed away, with inadequate appreciation of their total influence. Perhaps most significant among these obstacles is the impact of the media in which the perceived urgency of the daily news is permitted to dominate the decision-making agenda. Major network coverage of any particular trouble spot in the world can undermine a policymaker's determination to stay the course with respect to a well-thought-through, long-term strategy. Television helped get us into Somalia, and it later helped get us out. One is thus left without a convincing response to the question of why Somalia and why not Liberia (or any number of other equally pressing situations).

The media has such an impact, of course, because of the all-but-total fixation of most politicians on recent and soon-to-be-conducted public opinion polls. This kind of "leadership"—akin to steering a ship by watching its wake—works against developing the kind of vision needed to advance social change. Thus, the untoward impact of the media combined with the influence of public opinion polls is relegating policymaking to a largely reactive role.

The undue influence of organized special interest groups and political action committees in the financing of political campaigns also exacts a heavy toll. Though such bodies are typically chastised by most political aspirants, once in office, the noble criticisms soon fade and give way to a supine submission.

Beyond the above, leaders across the world must also respond to increasingly complex issues in ever shorter periods of time. Staggering advances in communication technologies coupled with information proliferation and accelerating international integration are changing the very nature of national decision-making and interactions among states. As a result, planning horizons are being compressed, longer-range considerations are being subordinated to the immediate, and integrated analysis is being overwhelmed by compartmentalized thinking. The potential for ill-considered decisions is rising correspondingly.

Should these trends continue, as they undoubtedly will, the danger arises that leaders will become managers, strategic thinking will be replaced by tactical considerations, and long-term planning will fall prey to immediate "triage" reactions. The implications of this assault on governance are ominous.

The range and prospective impact of these challenges, while intimidating, need not be paralyzing if properly acknowledged and addressed. As a useful first step, current and future administrations must be more deliberate and forceful in explaining to the public the basic interests that should guide U.S. foreign policy. One reason for recent limited public support has been the absence of any concerted effort to inspire it. In the president's 1996 State of the Union address, for example, foreign policy commanded a grand total of five minutes out of more than an hour of presentation.

Ordinarily, one might think of "principles" as being the more appropriate guideposts for foreign policy. Interests are sometimes difficult to calculate, while principles are inherently more generic and enduring. Unfortunately a number of the principles that served to guide us during the Cold War are difficult to pursue in today's more complicated environment. For example, where does one draw the line on the right of secession when even parts of cities seek their independence (as recently experienced in Russia), or on the right of refuge when immigration becomes too burdensome (as with Haiti)? How far should we go in advancing the Western view of human rights when other cultures may put a different weight on what is best for the community vis-à-vis the individual? And how does one reconcile the over-aggressive pursuit of this principle in dealing with other states with that of not interfering in their internal affairs?

A principle with too many exceptions begins to lose its meaning as a rule of conduct. Thus one is largely left with pursuing such principles on a situational basis, weighing which is the more important at a given time in a given set of circumstances. This even holds true when applying the general principles of engagement and enlargement to which the United States currently subscribes (as enunciated by President Clinton in his recent National Security Strategy reports). Further qualifications are needed if these principles are to be useful in determining in which situations the United States should or should not intervene.

A useful starting point might be to act first in those situations where U.S. principles, values, and interests coincide. Beyond that, the next most helpful litmus test might be to weigh any potential intervention against a predetermined set of considerations to be taken into account when such situations arise. Among other possibilities, such a set might include (1) the scale of the crisis, (2) our capacity to make a difference, (3) the relative effectiveness of unilateral action vs. acting in partnership with others, (4) the probable costs in both lives and money, and (5) the impact of our intervention on the interests and attitudes of other nations and people in the region.

Although there is an understandable tendency to want a hard and fast set of criteria for determining when to intervene, the consensus of the Steering Committee is that it is the president's role to define the criteria on a case-by-case basis and to sell his or her decision to the American public. In this regard, any foreign policy, to be sustainable, will have to play to the nature of the American public as a people—combining realism with idealism—and, wherever possible, be based on cost-benefit arguments that demonstrate how that policy best serves the United States over the long term.

The same requirement for public acceptance holds true for this report. In the final analysis, policymakers will only be able to do what the American people will support. The public's ability to comprehend and support arguments such as those set forth here should not be underestimated. What is key is serious, informed, articulate, and consistent leadership.

Foreign policy leadership in the future will require a much greater expenditure of effort in winning public approval for proposed policies. It will also place a high premium on our ability to develop common ideas and approaches in partnership with other nations. Even today, one is hard-pressed to think of any serious international challenge that can be fully met on a unilateral basis. Moreover, with the relentless march of technology, today's interdependence is but a faint shadow of that which is to come. Despite whatever disillusionment may have recently taken hold with regard to multilateral approaches to problem-solving, coalition leadership will be the sine qua non of a successful U.S. foreign policy in the years ahead.

On a final and summarizing note, the end of the Cold War has changed the nature of international politics, with the United States left in a more influential position relative to any other nation-state than at any time in its past. In the months and years ahead, the United States should use that influence to promote a closer political, economic, and security integration with Europe and Asia. On neither front should a hostile power be permitted to dominate.

At the next level, the United States should use its influence to enhance economic performance in regions that are vital to its interests and to maintain the peace, containing aggressive states as appropriate. In the less-developed world, the call is for exerting effective leadership in shaping international solutions to international problems.

More than any other industrialized country, the United States has the most at stake in a stable international order. If we do not take the lead in producing that stability, it is unlikely that anyone else can or will. That is a reality to which we must soon adjust.

U.S. Post–Cold War Strategy in Asia

Working Group on Asia

Richard Solomon, *chair**
William Clark
Richard Fairbanks
Banning Garrett*
Gerrit Gong
Stephen Solarz

* *principal authors*

U.S. Post–Cold War Strategy in Asia

No region of the world beyond North America is more vital to the future of the United States than the Asia-Pacific. And perhaps the future of no other region will hinge as much on the character and extent of U.S. engagement. A visionary and active United States that wisely marshals its resources to implement a long-term engagement strategy could continue to provide the glue that holds the region together while the United States helps shape a new post–Cold War regional order that protects and advances U.S. interests. In the last few years, however, many Asians have doubted the staying power of the United States despite the U.S. government's repeated public commitment to remaining a major power in the region.

The Asia-Pacific region on the eve of the twenty-first century presents U.S. policymakers with a panoply of contradictions. The region is more stable and peaceful now than at any time in this century. The region is experiencing an unprecedented explosion of economic growth, integration, and prosperity that is moving the center of the world economy toward the Pacific. Regional states are seeking to establish a level of multilateral economic, political, and security cooperation never seen in the region's often violent history.

At the same time, the post–Cold War strategic landscape in the Asia-Pacific region is being influenced by lingering conflicts, reemergent rivalries, and new security challenges—all of which are creating uncertainty and anxiety about the future. Unresolved territorial disputes and resentments that are the residue of past conflicts could exacerbate political tensions and become flash points for conflicts involving major states in the region. Efforts by political leaders in Asia-Pacific states to manage international economic, political, and security disputes are increasingly hampered by divisive domestic politics, national parochialism, and ethnocentrism. Finally, transpacific trade imbalances, disputes over market access, and differences over human rights strain political relations between the United States and key Asian states.

With the end of the Cold War division of the world, the yardstick for measuring the global and regional balances of power has changed. While military and strategic factors continue to be important, economic strength and technological development have gained ascendancy as critical elements in assessments of comprehensive national power. The strategically significant balances of power are regional more than global, and these balances are now shifting more rapidly than in the past, especially in response to the rising and falling economic fortunes of nations. This trend is particularly apparent in the Asia-Pacific region, where changes in the balance of power have been as significant, if less dramatic, as those

43

in Europe. Moscow's influence has declined precipitously while China and Japan have emerged as the key East Asian powers. Moreover, China's economic takeoff represents one of the most rapid ascents to major power status in history with as yet unclear implications for the reordering of international relations in the Asia-Pacific region and, indeed, the world.

To successfully manage its relations with Asia-Pacific states, the United States must appreciate the changes in the international politics of the region, including the relative increase in the power and confidence of the states of the region. Washington will have to recognize that responding to this growing confidence of the Asian states will require ever more extensive consultations at the most senior levels of government in order to effectively manage areas of dispute and develop areas of common interest.

Washington's ability to interact effectively with the two major regional powers, China and Japan, will be pivotal to future stability in the region. The United States' bilateral relationships with Beijing and Tokyo will have a major, perhaps decisive, impact on the future regional roles played by China and Japan and on the evolution of Sino-Japanese relations. Beijing and Tokyo each see their interests best served by the other power maintaining stable relations with the United States. China, for example, is concerned that a weakening or termination of the U.S.-Japan security relationship would encourage Japan to develop an independent military power that would threaten Chinese security interests and regional stability. Japan worries that the erosion of a positive relationship with China would exacerbate tendencies toward aggressive and destabilizing behavior by Beijing and impel the Chinese to accelerate their military buildup. At the same time, both China and Japan are also concerned about the possibility of collusion between the other power and the United States at its own expense. The Chinese are especially concerned that the United States and Japan may quietly cooperate to "contain" China.

These perspectives on the role of the United States underscore the essential function of the United States in maintaining the balance of power and stability in the Asia-Pacific region. The United States is viewed by regional states as the power with the greatest potential influence over the roles that China and Japan will play in the region. Regional states' fears of both China and Japan—as well as Japan's and China's fears of one another—have strengthened support in the region for the United States to play a balancing role through its continued military presence as well as its political leadership and economic engagement.

For the United States to play such a role in the Asia-Pacific region will require more than a material basis for the exercise of U.S. power or rhetorical assertions of a U.S. intent to remain engaged in the region's affairs. It will also depend on the credibility of U.S. leadership, which may be increasingly difficult to sustain in an era of domestically driven foreign policies and the growing assertion of special interests in the policymaking process. Defending short-run national or subnational economic interests untempered by a larger strategic vision, for example, may conflict with U.S. long-term economic and strategic interests in maintaining an open world economy and a cooperative international political system. Similarly, a

United States perceived as preoccupied with its domestic concerns and issues could lead Asians to lose confidence in U.S. leadership. As well, failure of the United States to maintain good working relations—and thus influence—with either or both China and Japan may adversely affect the willingness of regional states to rely on U.S. leadership.

☆ ASSESSMENT OF CHALLENGES IN THE ASIA-PACIFIC REGION

- **China's future may be uncertain, but its impact is inevitable.**   The biggest challenge facing the United States and the Asia-Pacific region is influencing the role and outlook of China, which is emerging as a major, perhaps eventually *the* major, power in East Asia. The challenge of managing the Taiwan issue and disputes with Beijing over trade, human rights, and proliferation is compounded by deepening mutual suspicions. Since the Nixon opening to Beijing in 1971, the Chinese leadership has sustained a strategic vision of China's interests that includes the necessity of maintaining good relations with the United States. With growing doubts in China about U.S. intentions toward China's emergence as a great power, there is a danger that Chinese leaders could adjust Beijing's national strategy to reduce the importance of good relations with Washington. The Chinese have become increasingly convinced that the strategic goal of the United States is to thwart China's emergence as a great power and to keep China weak and divided. Many people in the United States are similarly becoming increasingly suspicious of China's long-term intentions with respect to how it will use its growing economic strength and its status as a potentially well-armed economic superpower in the next century. The two sides face the danger of creating self-fulfilling prophecies if Beijing concludes that it must take steps to counter a perceived U.S. containment strategy and if Washington judges China's policies and actions as aimed at pushing the U.S. military out of Asia and exerting Chinese regional hegemony.

China's emergence as a great power need not be unduly disruptive or destabilizing. Beijing seeks a prolonged period of peace and stability in which to sustain its economic takeoff. The United States and China will have to demonstrate exceptional diplomatic skill and political restraint, however, in dealing with their bilateral differences over human rights, trade proliferation, and, perhaps most challenging, the complexities of Taiwan's search for greater international recognition and Beijing's determination to prevent Taiwan from gaining independence. While the international arms sales policies of the United States and China continue to be a serious source of contention in their bilateral relations, their common interests in non-proliferation—if managed well—could be developed as a source of cooperation between Beijing and Washington. Both countries have already recognized a common objective in defusing North Korea's nuclear weapons program and avoiding a renewed period of warfare on the peninsula. And in bilateral relations, the March 1995 agreement on protection of intellectual property rights (IPR) and market access has shown that the United States and China can reach agreement on thorny economic issues through hard, if sometimes rancorous, bargaining. The IPR agreement has prevented further deterioration of relations over trade issues, although tension over economic issues is likely to be a permanent feature of Sino-American relations that will need to be carefully managed.

The United States and China stepped back from the brink of confrontation over Taiwan in March 1996 and sought to resolve outstanding disputes on trade and proliferation while rekindling a strategic dialogue and trying to develop a framework for managing bilateral differences without provoking crises in Sino-American relations. The spring 1996 reversal of the downturn in ties between Washington and Beijing was brought about in part by a long-overdue high-level focus by the Clinton administration on relations with China, including a commitment to engage in frequent high-level dialogue and hold Sino-U.S. summits in 1997. The Taiwan crisis also seems to have helped catalyze a bipartisan consensus in the United States on the need to pursue a broad engagement strategy with China despite our differences and to avoid gratuitous punishment of the Chinese on human rights, trade, proliferation, and other contentious issues.

China also faces a number of fundamental domestic problems with potentially global consequences. The country's astounding economic growth coupled with its demographic expansion and ravenous consumption of energy and other natural resources will eventually present unprecedented challenges to Asia and the rest of the world. If China's per capita consumption of energy reaches that of South Korea, for example, the added damage to the environment (polluting emissions, global warming, acid rain, etc.) would be massive. China is already experiencing a shortage of clean water for most of its cities because of the billions of tons of industrial waste now being dumped into waterways. At the same time, the quantity and quality of arable land have declined as a result of rapid industrial expansion and infrastructure development. China will need to more than double its grain output over the next 20 years in order to feed its growing population. If this demand is not met, the country will be forced to import grain in an amount up to or surpassing the current grain production of the United States. Moreover, China's failure to sustain rapid economic growth in the face of its massive economic resource scarcity and environmental problems could lead to a political crisis with potentially disastrous consequences for regional and even global security.

• **Japan's regional role is likely to broaden.**   Japan's future and its regional role are relatively more predictable than those of China. Japan is likely to remain politically conservative and stable despite the process of political reform that began in 1993. In addition, Japan will be the leading East Asian economic power for the foreseeable future even if China's GNP surpasses Japan's total economic output. Japan has the capability to sustain a strong position in the regional balance of power—but not to emerge as the dominant power of the region—unless China disintegrates into political and economic chaos and American regional influence diminishes sharply.

Japan is in transition from an inward-looking nation, single-mindedly focused on expanding exports under the umbrella and tutelage of the U.S.-Japan security treaty, to a nation willing to play a larger global and regional role aimed at taking responsibility for international peace and stability in equal partnership with the United States. Many people in Japan remain committed to the post–war conception of Japan as a pacifist nation, irrevocably forswearing the use of force in international relations. Yet most Japanese officials and foreign/defense policy analysts now support a larger global and regional role for Japan in political and security affairs despite the current limitations imposed by domestic parochialism and Japan's "Peace Constitution." But they do not envision Japan playing an international role independent of the United States. Rather, they agree on the overriding importance to Japan's security of strengthening and broadening the U.S.-Japan security relationship in the post–Cold War era.

The extent and nature of Japan's future regional and global role will also be affected by the impact of Tokyo's "two steps forward, one step back" efforts to improve its image with Asian states. These countries remain suspicious of Japanese intentions due to Tokyo's failure to fully account for its crimes in World War II, despite Prime Minister Tomiichi Murayama's apology for Japan's actions on the occasion of the 50th anniversary of the end of the war in August 1995. Japan is thus likely to be content to "lead from behind" in East Asia, preferring to shelter its commercial and security interests in close collaboration with American strategic leadership.

The United States must make special efforts to sustain the U.S.-Japan alliance as the key relationship in the region if the United States is to successfully maintain the regional balance of power and the U.S. strategic position. Washington and Tokyo must refocus on the strategic importance and common interests of their "global partnership" and articulate a long-term vision of the security relationship that places bilateral economic differences in a more manageable political context on both sides of the Pacific. The Declaration on the Alliance in the Twenty-First Century signed by President Clinton and Prime Minister Hashimoto in Tokyo April 17, 1996, was a beginning in this effort. The next challenge will be to revise the 1978 Guidelines on Defense Cooperation without deepening regional suspicions of Japan's intentions.

Economic disputes will continue to threaten the fabric of the overall relationship as long as Japan runs massive trade surpluses with the United States and appears to remain recalcitrant in the face of demands that it open its markets to foreign goods and services. Both countries, however, share fundamental interests in preserving international stability and maintaining an open global trading system, as well as preventing domination of East Asia by a hostile power, halting North Korea's nuclear weapons program, and preventing a regional arms race.

- **Russia's influence in East Asia continues to decline.**   Russia's future impact on the stability of the Asia-Pacific region is another uncertain factor facing the

United States and regional leaders. The disintegration of the Soviet Union and the economic decline and political weakness of Russia have dramatically shifted the balance of power globally and regionally. Russia no longer poses an imminent threat to the region nor is Moscow a major regional actor. As a weak economic power, Russia is not a significant contributor to either the economic conflicts and dislocations that plague international relations in the region or the economic dynamism and growth that is integrating the Asia-Pacific. The role of Russia, and of U.S. strategic concern about Russia in the new security environment, is thus much more limited than in the past. Although Moscow's cooperation will be important in efforts to resolve the conflict on the Korean peninsula, Russia's chronic political instability and its sliding economy suggest that it will be quite some time before Russia reemerges as a major player in the economic and political life of the Asia-Pacific region.

Russia nevertheless could be a spoiler if its economic and security interests are ignored, or if it perceives regional states to have hostile intentions. The unresolved dispute with Japan over the southern Kuril Islands/Northern Territories continues to be a source of tension between Tokyo and Moscow that complicates development of more cooperative relations among Northeast Asian states. Although Russia's ties with China are more normal and have been bolstered by recent border agreements and confidence-building measures, the possibility exists that underlying mutual suspicion between the two countries could, in the long run, fuel renewed tensions between Moscow and Beijing. Perhaps most threatening to regional peace and stability would be the rise to power in Russia of ultranationalist or communist leaders specifically seeking to resurrect the Soviet empire and pursue territorial claims—or ambitions—at the expense of Asian states, although Boris Yeltsin's reelection as president in July 1996 has eased near-term concern about such a prospect. General uncertainties about Russia's future political and military policies even provide an impetus for China to maintain normal relations with the United States. In short, the calculus of the "strategic triangle" persists, at least in the minds of Chinese (and perhaps certain Russian) leaders.

- **A reunified Korea will change the regional balance of power in the twenty-first century.** The Korean peninsula poses the greatest near-term threat to regional security. The peninsula could once again move toward a crisis if the October 21, 1994, U.S.-DPRK (Democratic People's Republic of Korea) Framework Agreement collapsed, North Korea stepped up its nuclear weapons program, and the United States again sought UN sanctions. North Korean success in attaining a nuclear weapons status would undermine U.S. global efforts to halt proliferation of weapons of mass destruction, severely weaken the Nuclear Non-Proliferation Treaty (NPT) regime, and possibly provoke Japan and South Korea into building their own nuclear weapons. A regional nuclear weapons race would likely destabilize relations among regional states and create a political crisis that undermined confidence in the regional economy. Even if the Framework Agreement is implemented, North Korea, with more than one million troops, mostly forward-deployed and backed by artillery capable of striking Seoul, will continue to pose a serious military threat to the South (and U.S. troops there).

At the same time, the North Korean economy is facing a serious crisis—including potential widespread famine—while the stability of the country's political leadership is uncertain. The United States and South Korea should plan for the possibility that the North Korean regime could collapse at any time during the next few years, or that large refugee flows would impose great burdens on neighboring states. It is possible that the North may engage in a process of gradual economic reform that reverses the sharp decline in the economy and saves the Pyongyang regime, although the rigidity and divisions within the leadership make such a development unlikely. Such a process, however, would be met with relief by many South Koreans, who hope for a prolonged reunification process during which the North begins to improve its economic conditions to ensure a "soft landing," thus easing the burden that will ultimately fall on the South. In any case, Korea presents difficult challenges and opportunities for stabilizing initiatives under U.S. leadership.

For now, South Korea's regional role continues to be restricted by its overriding concern about the threat from North Korea and the problems of the pre-reunification period. Even during the reunification process, Korea is likely to be inwardly focused on the challenges and costs of some form of accommodation or absorption. Once this process is well-established, however, a united Korea may emerge as an economic powerhouse in the area. Moreover, the government of a reunified Korea will inherit a military establishment of more than 1.5 million troops and vast amounts of military hardware, necessitating a rethinking of the strategic calculus of the region. In addition, it is quite possible that a unified, nationalistic Korea will focus on its historical grievances against Japan, thus aggravating regional tensions and complicating U.S. alliances and relations with both powers. In the past year, China has moved to cultivate close relations with the government in Seoul—perhaps in anticipation of an eventual U.S. withdrawal from the peninsula or strained U.S.-ROK relations over policy for dealing with the North. The United States must make special efforts to sustain its close alliance ties to South Korea, as well as to support quiet efforts currently under way in Japan and South Korea to defuse historic enmity and strengthen economic ties.

- **ASEAN is an emerging power center—with limits.** In recent years, closer economic and political cooperation among regional states has been fostered by the Association of Southeast Asian States (ASEAN). Comprising Thailand, Malaysia, the Philippines, Singapore, Indonesia, Brunei, and Vietnam, ASEAN will likely expand in time to include Laos, Cambodia, and Myanmar. ASEAN's primary strategic concern is that neither China nor Japan emerge as regional hegemons—a goal that complements U.S. efforts in the area. Drawing China into a regional security dialogue through the ASEAN Regional Forum (ARF) is viewed by ASEAN leaders as a significant step toward ameliorating regional tensions. The deep political, cultural, and historical differences among the ASEAN countries, however, and their huge discrepancies in size and population make it unlikely that ASEAN will operate as a unified actor in the region. In the long run, ASEAN is likely to have an influential voice in regional affairs but will not be a primary actor on the scale of the United States, Japan, or China.

- **The rising economic and strategic importance of South Asia.**   In the early 1990s, South Asian governments began implementing reforms to accelerate economic growth. Throughout the region, countries have taken steps to deregulate industry and commerce, liberalize trade, reform financial markets, and increase foreign investment. These initial reforms have achieved positive results, including increased foreign exchange reserves, growing exports, and rising foreign investment. India, and to a lesser extent Pakistan, Sri Lanka, and Bangladesh (all of which have embarked on market-oriented reforms of their own), have the potential to turn South Asia into a premier regional market and major destination for industry, light manufacturing, high technology, and services. We have seen other cooperative reform efforts result from meetings of the South Asian Association for Regional Cooperation (SAARC). These have heralded both the submission of potential goods for inter-regional trade and the long-awaited implementation of a South Asia Preferential Trading Agreement (SAPTA).

  The issue of nuclear proliferation in India and Pakistan has taken on particular significance lately, with both countries still refusing to participate in the renewal of the NPT. The dangers inherent in relations between India and Pakistan cannot be taken lightly. The two countries have already fought three wars, and a proxy war between Pakistan-sponsored militants and Indian security forces rages on in Indian Kashmir. Inflexible attitudes and policies on both sides aggravate serious tensions, tensions enhanced by the alleged possession of a nuclear capability by both countries. India's successful development of a ballistic missile system and Pakistan's alleged acquisition of M-11 missile technology from China could destabilize the regional security balance. If Indo-Pakistani relations turn for the worse, both countries could assemble a limited number of nuclear warheads in a relatively short time, and both possess missiles capable of delivering the warheads. As such, South Asia is an area where regional conflicts have the potential to escalate to a nuclear exchange.

- **The possibility of regional arms races and the proliferation of weapons of mass destruction.**   Many Western analysts have expressed concern that a new conventional arms race may be beginning in Asia. There are many domestic as well as international factors fueling defense budget increases and the buildup of military forces by regional states. These include military modernization cycles of many of the armed forces in the region; rising affluence of regional states, enabling them to afford high-technology weapons systems; a "buyer's market," especially for weapons sold at fire-sale prices by the former Soviets; and a shift from a military focus on counterinsurgency to concern about defending national territory, especially territorial waters, which requires larger and more capable naval and air forces as well as improved surveillance, command, control, and communications capabilities. Regional arms buildups are also driven by mistrust among regional states and fear that the United States will withdraw its forces from the region.

The primary impetus for nuclear proliferation in the region is the prospect of North Korea acquiring nuclear weapons, which is a Korea-specific phenomenon that is being addressed by the U.S.-North Korea Framework Agreement. Asia-Pacific states have been lax, however, in joining or ratifying global arms control agreements, including the Chemical Weapons Convention and the Biological Weapons Convention. In addition, Japan's accumulation of plutonium for commercial purposes raises the prospect of creating a regional "Asiatom" authority to manage the reprocessing and storage of potential weapons-grade nuclear materials to build confidence among Northeast Asian states, especially about Japan's intentions.

☆ POLITICAL AND ECONOMIC TRENDS INFLUENCING SECURITY MANAGEMENT

The ability of nations to manage the stresses produced by increasing economic integration and interdependence may be weakened by the decline in sovereignty of the nation state over financial and political affairs as well as by chronically weak political leadership that is unable to make the hard choices in support of long-term national interests. Concerns such as environmental degradation, shrinking per capita resource bases, demographic explosions, and the weakening of national and state institutions could also provide new challenges to regional as well as global stability. Some of the trends that will complicate regional security management include the following:

- **The growing importance of economics to stability and security.** Security and economics have become even more intertwined as the importance of technological and commercial factors in setting national priorities and determining the balance of power has increased in the last decade. International economic integration reduces the incentive of states to use military force to resolve conflicts, and it increases their stakes in maintaining a stable and peaceful trading order. These trends can also contribute to instability, however, by increasing states' vulnerability to the actions of other states and the vagaries of their economic performance. Moreover, as indicated by China's apparent willingness to put at risk its economic modernization by using force against Taiwan should it declare independence, there is a limit to the inhibitions on military conflict provided by economic interdependence.

An economic downturn in the Asia-Pacific region, perhaps produced by a global recession or inter-regional trade wars, could also have serious effects on regional stability, including (1) devolution of China into economic crisis and political chaos, with massive flows of refugees into neighboring states, and even loss of central command and control of Chinese nuclear weapons; (2) undermining the ability of Tokyo and Washington to successfully manage U.S.-Japanese relations as well as to cooperate in addressing regional security issues; (3) increasing tensions among Southeast Asian countries fighting for shrinking markets and blaming each other for their economic hardships; (4) weakening the ability and desire of regional states to integrate emerging market economies such as Vietnam into the international system; (5) increasing the support for regional protectionist trade blocs as well as increasing tensions among the potential participants in such an exclusionary trading system; and (6) producing potentially disruptive shifts in the balance of power in response to changing economic fortunes as some nations rise and others fall behind. At the same time, continued economic growth in the region will not necessarily strengthen the ability of regional states to cooperate or to mitigate the political impact of their economic differences.

- **Conflicts and mistrust inhibit regional integration and cooperation.**   The history of conflict, animosity, and suspicion among Asian-Pacific states is, unfortunately, a major impediment to close political integration. There is almost no history of cooperative regional mechanisms, and ethnic or cultural differences stand in the way of close association, despite the promotion by some leaders of "Asian values" as a basis for regional cooperation.

National parochialism also vies with internationalism in shaping nations' postures toward the outside world. It is masked in today's world of a rapidly growing regional economic "pie." Hence, in a time of economic contraction, the narrow, inward focus of Asia's societies and subnational groups could re-emerge to undermine today's trend toward a broader, more expansive and inclusive world view. For many of the nations of East Asia, the difficult history of their interactions has left a residue of resentments, animosities, and fears that reinforce cultural and nationalist barriers to closer cooperation in a "New Pacific Community." Even in Southeast Asia, where the states have a recent history of cooperation under ASEAN, mutual suspicions and huge differences in geographic size and population diminish the prospects for European-style unity.

In the long run, further integration in the Asia-Pacific region will be constrained by the huge disparities in size, population, wealth, and technological level among the states, especially the overwhelming size and population of China, as well as by geography and politics. The countries of the region do not form a contiguous geographical region that would foster cross-border movement of people and goods. Nor are the relatively homogenous and ethnocentric societies of East Asia especially open to immigration and co-option of people from neighboring states as called for in the creation of a unified Europe. The region also lacks a common political tradition and visionary political leadership to overcome the parochialism of domestic populations and the mistrust between nations and peoples. Moreover, Asian countries are highly resistant to economic or political integration that would reduce their sphere of national sovereignty.

- **Chronic weakness hinders political leadership.**   The diffusion of power within states and the weakening of state sovereignty are creating weak political leadership that exacerbates the challenge of managing the problems of the region. There is no reason to expect more consistently decisive policymaking and implementation in the future unless there are major crises, including military conflicts, that lead people to rally behind their national leaders. In the meantime, efforts by nations to cooperate in their collective self-interest to manage regional economic, political, and security issues will be continually hobbled by the inability of political leaders to adopt and implement policies they know are in their own state's long-term best interest.

- **The promise and limits of multilateralism.**   U.S. management of the twenty-first century security challenges in the Asia-Pacific may be supplemented by a range of bilateral and multilateral approaches rather than by one overarching strategy, such as containment, or one security structure. Resolution of most territorial disputes, including the Japanese-Russian contest over the southern Kuril Islands, will likely be confined to bilateral processes. Threats such as North Korea's nuclear weapons program will be best managed through a combination of bilateral negotiations and ad hoc, U.S.-led "crisis-management multilateralism" that includes close consultations with the relevant regional powers. In the longer run, the transition in Korea may be facilitated by a "Northeast Asia Security Dialogue."

The possibility of regional arms races should be mitigated through bilateral security dialogues between regional states—such as the ASEAN Regional Forum—as well as by U.S.-supported "trust-building multilateralism." The latter includes security discussions, greater military transparency, and reciprocated unilateral steps to reduce perceived threats as advocated by nongovernmental organizations (NGOs) such as the Council on Security Cooperation in the Asia Pacific (CSCAP) and its American affiliate, USCSCAP. The ASEAN Regional Forum, the South Asian Association for Regional Cooperation, and the Asia-Pacific Economic Cooperation forum (APEC), along with other organizations aimed at increasing multilateral cooperation in the region, have already begun to contribute to easing tensions, building trust, and managing economic, political, and security relations among regional states.

APEC is the primary U.S. vehicle to promote regional economic cooperation. APEC's main contribution to regional stability lies in its efforts to establish an Asia-Pacific free trade zone and to bring about closer integration through frequent senior leadership meetings that are helping to create a common agenda, shared perspectives and policies on some issues, and a basis for managing potential or actual conflicts. APEC has also been an important tool for the United States to pursue its goals of reducing trade barriers and otherwise advancing U.S. economic interests in the region. Despite wide participation in APEC, however, APEC's influence over the region is likely to be limited: APEC remains a loose forum for discussing economic cooperation—including unenforceable commitments to trade liberalization—and some of its members are even wary of establishing the forum as a formal organization.

The United States should have no illusions that economic, political, and security integration in the Asia-Pacific region will be sufficiently developed in the foreseeable future to form the basis for a NATO-like security community that provides an alternative to strong U.S. regional leadership, U.S. bilateral security ties with Japan and other states, and close cooperation—or a concert of powers—among the United States, China, and Japan (and in some cases, Russia). Multilateral cooperation is likely to evolve only slowly and with limited authority and power to address the long-term security concerns of the region, especially the future roles of the major powers. Nevertheless, by exercising a leadership role, Washington can shape multilateral approaches to enhancing regional security that complement the United States' bilateral security ties and forward military presence, and thus further exercise the balancing role that remains the key to regional stability.

☆ U.S. INTERESTS AND GOALS IN EAST ASIA AND THE PACIFIC

VITAL INTERESTS

- **To prevent any single power from dominating the region.**   The United States must continue to play a vital role in maintaining the balance of power in the Asia-Pacific region as it evolves toward a new pattern and structure of great power relations and regional cooperation. The chief challenges for the United States are (1) effectively integrating an increasingly powerful and assertive China into a stable international order in a way that is consonant with U.S., Chinese, and regional interests; (2) managing our complex and vital relationship with a Japan that is seeking to redefine its global and regional roles to reflect more accurately its growing economic and political power; and (3) maintaining the security of South Korea in the face of North Korea's nuclear weapons program and threatening conventional military capabilities, and facilitating a reunification process as North Korea copes with its economic and leadership crises.

- **To ensure continued commercial, political, and military access to and through the region.**   The United States has a vital interest in promoting and sustaining the economic development of the Asia-Pacific region and in preventing any combination of powers from de-linking the region from North America through exclusionary economic groupings or other means. This is not to suggest the United States should accept the status quo, with its large trade imbalances, but rather it should recognize that as national economies mature, regulatory frameworks and trading practices become increasingly standardized and trade imbalances are reduced. The United States should undertake any necessary actions to spur the economic development of our trading partners, while remaining aware of the limited effectiveness of pushing too hard.

The U.S. military presence in the region, welcomed by almost all regional states, is essential for maintaining the U.S. role in securing the sea and air lines of communication essential to global commerce, and for meeting U.S. defense requirements in the Indian Ocean and the Persian Gulf/Middle East regions. It is also the *bona fide* of U.S. assertions of its intent to remain engaged in East Asia, to maintain the regional balance of power, and to protect the interests of our allies. It is the core element—along with access to our domestic market—of being taken seriously in the region.

- **To prevent the proliferation of weapons of mass destruction, including nuclear weapons and ballistic missile technology as well as chemical and biological weapons and technology.**   The United States has a vital interest in halting the spread of weapons of mass destruction in the Asia-Pacific region, including the transfer of such weapons or weapons technology by North Korea and China. The United States also has a vital interest in preventing the acquisition of such weapons by other regional states, including South Korea, Japan, and Taiwan.

IMPORTANT INTERESTS

- **Observance of human rights norms.**   In a region resistant to pressures to accept "Western" human rights standards, it is important for the United States to develop multilateral approaches to the promotion of universal human rights, in part by encouraging the evolution of regimes that are increasingly democratic and observant of human rights. Such governments will be more likely to manage effectively and peacefully the increasing power generated by their dramatic economic growth. Support for human rights in U.S. foreign policy is also important for sustaining public support for U.S. involvement in the region. At the same time, we must handle this issue carefully to avoid deepening the rift between the United States and Asian states that are critical of purported attempts to "impose" Western values. Effective promotion of our human rights concerns remains a key challenge to the conduct of U.S. foreign policy. The use of multilateral mechanisms and the nurturing of indigenous Asian proponents of human rights observance are essential to this process.

- **Peaceful resolution of competing offshore territorial claims in the South China Sea.**   U.S. interest in a peaceful resolution of these potentially explosive international disputes may require that Washington play a quiet yet proactive role—backed by our defense commitments in the region—to encourage a negotiated resolution of competing claims. Failure to resolve the disputes could lead to a polarizing military confrontation with China, regional arms sales, or accommodation to Chinese power by the smaller states of the region at the expense of their relations with the United States.

- **Regional cooperation through multilateral forums.**   Sustaining the integrity of ASEAN is important for the maintenance of multilateral political and security cooperation that reinforces our bilateral treaty commitments. Support for yearly ASEAN post–ministerial dialogues and the ASEAN Regional Forum on security issues enables the United States to build multilateral consensus on foreign policy issues. Supporting APEC's plans for regional free trade furthers American trade goals, while providing all the positive aspects of increased economic integration and cooperation that extend beyond the sphere of trade itself.

BENEFICIAL INTERESTS

- **Ecological health of the region.**   Regional efforts to protect the environment undertaken largely by the states of East Asia themselves, either unilaterally or through multilateral initiatives (such as the drift-net fishing accord, pollution abatement measures, and efforts to prevent deforestation) should be supported by the United States.

☆ U.S. INTERESTS AND GOALS IN SOUTH ASIA

It is in the interest of the United States to form a broad, balanced, and integrated strategy toward South Asia that is sustainable over the long term, as this region will be increasingly vital to American welfare and security. South Asia's fate will increasingly influence the world with regard to economic growth, regional conflicts, environmental protection, the advancement of human rights, the rise of Islamic fundamentalism, narcotics trafficking, and terrorism. An American strategy toward the region should be based on the following key considerations:

VITAL INTERESTS

- **To ensure continued U.S. military, commercial, and political access to, as well as transit through, the region.**   The United States has a vital interest in preventing any one power or combination of powers from limiting U.S. access to the region through exclusionary economic groupings or other means.

- **To contain nuclear weapons and missile proliferation.**   Indo-Pakistani tensions in particular make South Asia an area with great potential for nuclear exchange. Preventing the further proliferation of nuclear weapons and missiles in the region is a vital interest, particularly if one considers the proximity of South Asia to China, Iran, and Central Asian countries.

IMPORTANT INTERESTS

- **Closer economic integration with the region.**   U.S. businesses stand to reap significant economic benefits from investment in South Asia, which represents a huge emerging market—India's middle class alone numbers more than 250 million people. The U.S. Commerce Department places India among the top 10 emerging markets. As such, U.S. foreign policy toward India and the region will be of paramount importance to the U.S. business community, which has taken the lead in investment in India. As India's biggest foreign investor and trading partner, the United States has a competitive advantage vis-à-vis European and Asian countries. South Asia's economic liberalization means the opportunity for more exports and thus more jobs for the United States.

- **Internal economic reforms and the development of regional economic forums.**   The United States has a long-term interest in promoting transitions to market economies in South Asia. Accelerated economic growth in India, Pakistan, and other South Asian countries, and the further integration of these countries into the world economy, should enhance regional and political stability. As such, the U.S. role is important in promoting the continuation of economic and political liberalization. This process should include the formation of a regional trading block under SAARC and ultimate integration of India and its regional partners into Asia through bilateral relationships with individual Asian countries, as well as ongoing dialogue and possible membership in forums such as ASEAN, APEC, and the Asia Free Trade Area (AFTA).

BENEFICIAL INTERESTS

- **Regional social development.**   The United States has an interest in the socio-economic development of South Asian countries. For instance, rapid population growth, urbanization, and industrialization in South Asia could exacerbate global warming and environmental degradation. U.S. assistance to South Asian countries through bilateral development aid and the cooperation of the U.S. government and NGOs in helping South Asian countries with their development challenges are essential in addressing population growth, poverty control, education, and environmental concerns.

- **Democracy and human rights norms.**   It is our intent to support democratic governments in the South Asian region through U.S.-South Asian exchanges involving NGOs, legislators, and human rights organizations. India and Sri Lanka are already established democracies, while neighbors, including Islamic Pakistan, are undergoing the process of democratization. This movement is ongoing despite ethnic, religious, and subnational conflicts. South Asia under democratic rule will bolster political stability and economic and social development, thus paving the way for peace in the region.

☆ POLICY RECOMMENDATIONS

- **Strengthen U.S. leadership in the Asia-Pacific region.**   The leading role of the United States in the Asia-Pacific region can be sustained and strengthened over the next decade if the United States seizes current and future opportunities to enhance its position. The United States should maintain a significant forward military presence in the region and nurture its alliance and security relationships with Japan, South Korea, and the states of ASEAN. In addition, the resurgent competitiveness of U.S. industry and its growing focus on the dynamic opportunities in the region, along with a desire of Asians to spur U.S. investment (to anchor America's regional commitment and to counterbalance other commercial powers, especially Japan), could lead to a growing U.S. economic presence relative to other powers.

No country in the region or elsewhere is likely in the foreseeable future to come close to matching the United States in comprehensive national power, including military, political, economic, diplomatic, technological, and cultural strength. To maintain its leadership, however, the United States must continue to demonstrate that it is the indispensable crisis manager in the region and a reliable guarantor of the security of its allies. This must hold true for the most recent Korean peninsula security initiative involving the United States, South and North Korea, Japan, and China, just as it was in negotiating the U.S.-North Korea Framework Agreement. While that agreement may be flawed, none of the other regional actors was in a position to negotiate an accord with North Korea and prevent Pyongyang from moving ahead with reprocessing spent fuel rods and producing tens of nuclear warheads.

Managing the impact of China's emergence as a great power will be the primary foreign policy challenge facing the United States and its allies. China's immense size and population, combined with its rapid economic growth and assertive use of military power—as was demonstrated in its "missile diplomacy" against Taiwan in early 1996—will give renewed relevance to the U.S.-Japan alliance for maintaining stability and confidence throughout Asia as the region adjusts to China's rising power and influence. Whether the U.S. position in the Asia-Pacific region will be maintained and strengthened—rather than eroded (with the current questioning of our staying power)—also depends on whether the United States can sustain moderate growth of its own economy and exercise wise political leadership in shaping the new order in Asia.

- **Integrate China into the international order.**   Fundamental to our future position in the region and to Asian stability and economic growth is the task of developing a strategic vision of U.S. interests. Such a vision should include a long-term strategy for achieving Washington's stated goal of integrating China into international economic, political, and security processes. Besides encouraging continued Chinese participation in regional multilateral consultative bodies such as APEC and the ASEAN Regional Forum, a longer-term objective should be creating conditions for including China in global management bodies such as the G-7. China must also become a member of the World Trade Organization (WTO) and international arms control arrangements regimes such as the Missile Technology Control Regime (MTCR). In the long run, China must be "present at the creation" of international regimes that set rules or guidelines that China is expected to follow. The United States must make clear to Beijing that participation in such arrangements is based on assuming responsibility for international order rather than the pursuit of narrow national interests and nationalistic concerns alone. The United States must argue convincingly that its interest in issues such as its access to the Chinese market and human rights are goals in themselves and not covert policies to weaken the Chinese government or thwart the country's economic development.

- **Avoid mutually reinforcing cycles of Sino-American suspicion.**   Today, Washington and Beijing are at a critical point where farsighted leadership has the potential to arrest the current downward spiral of deepening mutual suspicions and demonization that could lead to a new Cold War in Asia—or at the least a confrontational Sino-American relationship that would be extremely damaging to the interests of all states of the region.

- **Safeguard against a Sino-Taiwanese war.**   Special effort must be made now to reaffirm the political framework developed in the 1970s for managing the Taiwan issue. Beijing must be responsive to Taiwan's maturation and its desire for greater international recognition. The challenge to Beijing, Taipei, and Washington is to see that this happens within the "one China" policy framework laid down in the 1972 Sino-U.S. Shanghai Communiqué. Deft diplomacy will be required to keep the Taiwan Strait peaceful and to sustain positive U.S. relations with both the island and mainland China. The United States must stand by its commitments to China in the three Sino-American communiqués as well as implement the Taiwan Relations Act and respond to a changing domestic political scene in Taiwan. Washington should make it clear to both parties that they must work out a solution directly between themselves and that the United States will seek neither to prevent nor to mediate unification. Whatever the merits of allowing the president of Taiwan to make a "private" visit to the United States in June 1995, that decision unleashed a destabilizing series of developments, including a sharp downturn in Sino-American relations, a cut-off in the Taiwan-Mainland dialogue, stepped-up military exercises by Beijing including missile firings near Taiwan, and counter exercises by Taiwan. Washington's dispatch of two carrier battle groups to the Taiwan Strait area in response to the heightened tensions was essential to restabilizing the area and to sustaining the credibility of the U.S. security role in the region. U.S. policy on the Taiwan issue must be guided by a clear strategic vision that a military conflict in the Taiwan Strait would be disastrous for Taiwan, China, and Japan and that it is determined to support a peaceful resolution of Beijing's differences with Taipei. Regional peace and stability would be undermined, and the U.S. strategic position jeopardized, if Beijing were to assert its intention to achieve reunification with Taipei by force of arms.

- **Rekindle a U.S.-Japan "global partnership."**   A confrontational U.S. approach to opening Japan's economy—by setting quantitative measures for market penetration backed by the threat of sanctions—has produced meager results while heightening Japanese resentment of U.S. presence tactics. The United States should seek to put its commercial differences with Tokyo in the context of common interests and the strengthening of U.S.-Japan political and security ties, as President Clinton effectively did at his April 1996 summit meeting in Tokyo with Prime Minister Ryutaro Hashimoto. That said, Washington should continue to work with and encourage Japan to become a more open, consumer-oriented society through deregulation and liberalization of the Japanese economy—steps that would produce the economic growth needed to stimulate Japanese demands for U.S. goods and begin to reduce the U.S. trade deficit.

Washington and Tokyo need to focus on making a reality of the U.S.-Japan "global partnership." At the same time, Tokyo and Beijing must jointly address issues of regional and global security and engage in coordinated and complementary efforts to pursue long-term common interests, including unprecedented resource depletion and competition, looming food shortages, and environmental degradation and pollution.

- **Develop an integrative approach to South Asia's stability.**   Developing a broad and integrated strategy toward South Asia, which includes promoting rapid economic development in the region, will enable the United States to shift the region's prevailing focus from long-standing regional hostilities to greater regional cooperation, especially in regard to preventing further nuclear proliferation in the subcontinent.

The United States has decided to take a pragmatic rather than a confrontational approach in its efforts to convince India and Pakistan to give up nuclear weapons. The immediate focus of the United States should be to head off the deployment of ballistic missiles capable of carrying nuclear warheads and to avoid escalating nuclear and missile competition on the subcontinent.

It will be difficult to compel India and Pakistan to sign the NPT. The United States must continue its efforts to build mutual trust through measures such as cooperation in joint peacekeeping operations under the UN, dialogues on strategic issues, and increased military contacts. The United States must urge India and Pakistan to improve relations through dialogue on issues not related to Kashmir such as (1) a joint declaration on "no first use" of nuclear weapons; (2) a pull-back of troops from Siachen; and (3) programs on joint narcotics control. It should also seek ways to help "ripen" prospects for a political solution of the Kashmir situation.

Finally, the United States should provide further financial and technical support to SAARC and increase links between SAARC and other regional organizations such as ASEAN and APEC as a means for addressing long-standing regional disputes and for integrating South Asia into the international political and economic arenas.

Appendix B

The United States and Europe

Working Group on the United States and Europe

Richard Burt, *chair**

Stanton Burnett

Stephen Hadley

Max Kampelman

Robert Neumann

Simon Serfaty*

Anthony Smith

Don Snider

John Yochelson

* *principal authors*

The United States and Europe

TRENDS AND TENDENCIES

For Europe, the several years since the end of the Cold War have been largely disappointing. Western allies, who won the Cold War together, are faced with prospects of discord with one another and temptations of disengagement from each other. In eastern, central, and southeastern Europe, the collapse of Communism and the disintegration of the Soviet empire have brought back to life a European past that had been left for dead. In Bosnia, Chechnya, and elsewhere, the prolonged passivity of Western powers, including the United States, has resembled the failed policies of the inter-war years. Out of Russia, more belligerent tones have remained unanswered, and occasionally more bellicose actions have not been sufficiently condemned.

In Western Europe, the state of the European Union (EU) is fragile. The Treaty of Maastricht signed in December 1991 proved far too ambitious. The organization of a unified market ("Europe 92") has not brought the economic benefits that had been predicted. Plans to launch an economic and monetary union in 1997 have been postponed, and the new timetable set for 1999 is in doubt. Hopes that a common EU foreign and security policy could be forged promptly have faded. In sum, the momentum gathered after the end of the Cold War has flagged as populations have become more parochial and national capitals have reasserted their authority.

Nations, too, are in a fragile state. At the polls or in the courts, political elites are being dismissed en masse. High rates of unemployment have barely improved with the end of the longest and deepest economic recession suffered by Europe since 1945. Apprehensions about individual safety and resentment over the flows of immigrants from the east and the south are growing. Widespread corruption has become a matter of public concern. Everywhere, there seems to be a sense of national drift and even an air of decadence.

Finally, in the United States, too, priority has been placed on domestic issues, and the will or capacity for international leadership is fading. *Nunc demum redit animus*—now at last life returns to normal. But whose life and what normalcy? As past achievements are reviewed, the public appears to sense what would have been lost generally had the Cold War not been won, but few seem to understand specifically what was won by not losing it. As the fear of old enemies recedes, the appeal of old friends fades. As the West moves again from the unity it achieved in wartime to the discord often shown in peacetime, is the century ending with an American withdrawal from Europe?

Such gloom is, of course, premature. Existing trends are cause for concern, but they are by no means permanent. To be sure, the agenda that lies ahead is formidable, whether for the nation state or for any of the institutions to which these states belong or which they hope to join. After each war comes a period of uncertainty during which more effort is needed to sustain the unity of the victorious coalition.

But how can unity be achieved? The most immediate and most convincing answer has to do with the provision of leadership—especially from the United States. As the Bosnia settlement illustrates, in Europe as elsewhere there is no alternative to U.S. leadership. In the absence of continued U.S. assertiveness, instability will be contagious—especially when it occurs in the vicinity of Russia, whose empire is gone but whose imperial inclinations remain. Conflicts that go unanswered and appear to make aggression pay do matter—now, for those who are victimized, and, later, for those who sat idly by on the sidelines.

In short, coming out of the Cold War the United States must continue to assert the role it assumed on the Continent, however reluctantly, after 1945. Europe presents the United States with a unique combination of geopolitical, economic, and sociocultural interests. After the Cold War, the totality of these interests remains vital to our security.

☆ VITAL INTERESTS

American geopolitical interests still center on opposition to the dominance of the region by any adversarial power. As the century ends, a stable balance in the Old World remains elusive without the New World. Left to itself, Europe is too weak for Russia (whose power must be balanced) and even Germany (whose security must be sustained). Only the United States can reassure either state against the other, and all states against both. It is not too early to remember the consequences of the absence of such reassurances after World War I—and under what conditions. It is not too late to remember the conditions under which these reassurances were extended after World War II—and with what consequences. Beyond the Cold War, the U.S. withdrawal from the Continent would open Europe to the dangers of renationalization—that is, a return to the competitive diplomatic and security practices that, in the past, have often ended badly.

As suggested above, the problems posed by Russia and post–Cold War Germany, while linked, are dramatically different. Russia appears to be getting back on its feet geopolitically before it is back on its feet economically. As a result, past fixtures of the Cold War agenda are reemerging, including Russia's coercion of its neighbors (in the Caucasus and central Asia), its influence in the Gulf (including its proposed nuclear exports to Iran), its activism on behalf of traditional allies in the Balkans, and its threat to break out of the Conventional Forces in Europe (CFE) Treaty. The rapid reemergence of these issues, among others, underscores the persistence of geopolitics in Europe and, more specifically, the continuing need for a transatlantic security framework that keeps America directly involved in the defense of Europe.

A transatlantic security framework is also a necessary part of preserving European stability after German reunification. Here the goal is not, as in the case of Russia, to maintain the balance of power on the Continent. Instead, it is to preserve a multilateral security system in Europe in which Germany feels safe and thus free of any temptation to explore alternative security arrangements. Again, direct U.S. military engagement in European defense is vital to keeping Germany tied into Western security arrangements.

In this context, then, the North Atlantic Treaty Organization (NATO) remains the institution most directly responsible for Europe's security and for the security of U.S. interests in Europe. Its preservation can be considered a vital interest in and of itself. NATO is the primary instrument available to the United States to enlist allies of means and substance to perform five critical functions:

- deter new outbursts of Russian military power, moderate renewed expressions of Russia's geopolitical ambitions, and, on this basis, engage Russia in constructive cooperation;
- consolidate Germany's place in the Western security structure;
- guarantee the independence of the former members of the Warsaw Pact;
- deter and contain future small wars in Europe; and
- respond to such global interests as the spread of terrorism and the proliferation of arms of mass destruction.

The case, however, against either a U.S. withdrawal or substantial draw-down from Europe is not only about security—the preservation, that is, of one's national self and that of other countries with which we may have or feel much in common. The case against withdrawal is also about the economic and political ties that have been built over the years.

Some argue that political and economic ties matter less than before because emerging markets in Asia and Latin America have more potential for growth than Europe's economies, or because population shifts are moving the United States east and southward. In fact, over the past decade neither the flows of direct investment nor the rates of trade expansion toward Europe relative to other parts of the world confirms this argument. Moreover, neither the political nor the economic conditions that prevail in Western Europe and Asia would appear to make irreversible trends that appear to favor the latter relative to the former. And even if they were irreversible, the U.S. presence in, and identification with, Europe has become so wide and so deep as to transcend the arithmetic of troop deployment or the accounting of commercial transactions.

☆ IMPORTANT INTERESTS

It is not just history that has moved on since 1949, when the United States overcame its objections to entering an alliance outside the Western Hemisphere in peacetime. Geography, too, has moved as the scope and diversity of America's entanglement with Europe have created an increasingly common economic and political space across the Atlantic. Now the United States stands as a de facto non-member-state of the European Union—with a population of its own living in a single market that receives $110 billion worth of U.S. annual exports (including especially manufactured goods, and often conducive to a trade surplus) and hosts about $250 billion of U.S. direct investment responsible for more than $850 billion of sales and $30 billion of corporate earnings every year.

Thus, an important U.S. interest is to nurture in Europe an environment that is economically dynamic and politically stable. This goal can be achieved most effectively with a European Union that is

- open, flexible, and competitive in economic structure and practice;
- democratic and compatible with the social values and polices that prevail in the United States;
- resistant to protectionist pressures for selected sectors;
- open to economic and political ties with its neighbors in the East, beginning with the countries of Central Europe; and
- responsive to the need for a "special relationship" with the United States.

Finally, as Western values are under assault in and from other regions, cultural and historical affinities that link both sides of the Atlantic must also help overcome passing commercial rivalries and political divergences. To be sure, many of the values shared by the United States and the states of Europe are universal; assuming a Western monopoly for any one of them would be offensive to the rest of the world. Yet the meaning commonly given to these values, the political philosophy that underlines them, and the individual commitments made by citizens to respect them are especially common across the Atlantic—among countries that have come from a Euro-Atlantic community of values as well as one of interests. In an era in which cultural differences will often assume political meaning, these values should not be compromised.

The United States and the states of Europe must preserve and strengthen the common political, economic, and cultural space they created in Europe and across the Atlantic during the Cold War. This is the challenge of continuity. But they must also help expand this space to other states that belong to similar traditions and are seeking membership now that the Cold War is over. This is the challenge of change.

Relative to its past, Western Europe has become rather peaceful and affluent. The reason has to do with the organization of a space *communautaire* that stands as one of the most notable legacies of the Cold War. In the comfort of this space, the former European Great Powers (except Turkey and Russia) are grouped in a political union that denies its members the full sovereignty in the name of which they waged many of their wars in the past.

This peaceful transformation of Western Europe is a historical achievement that was made possible by the United States, whose enlightened postwar policies gave the states of Europe the time they needed to forget and the aid they needed to recover. Whether geopolitically or economically, the union of Europe has served America generally well, and it should continue to be encouraged. But as the current debate underscores, a united Europe means different things to different Europeans, and to Americans.

In coming years, as in the past, "building Europe" will remain up to the European states themselves; but the influence exerted by the United States on the form and pace of the construction should not be underestimated. So long as "Europe" is unfinished and so long as its members continue to disagree over the final architecture of the edifice that they seek, America's political dialogue with Europe, as well as Europe's dialogue with America, will continue to have a significant states-to-state dimension—including, admittedly, some bilateral relationships that are more "special" than others, whether transatlantic (including the United States and Britain) or intra-European (including France and Germany). This principle will be made even more true if we quietly urge EU countries known for their skepticism toward the Union (like Britain) to move on with the construction of Europe, and if, at the same time, EU states known for their skepticism toward NATO (like France) work toward closer EU ties with the United States.

In this context, consultation across the Atlantic before final decisions are made should be improved. To fulfill this goal, the EU will have to make space for the United States in all its institutional settings, and all branches of the U.S. government will have to upgrade their relations with the EU at all levels: with the Commission (acting as the EU's chief executive) and its various directorates, with the Council of Ministers and its many committees, with the European Parliament (viewed as Europe's main legislative body), and even with the European Court of Justice.

Moving into the twenty-first century, a treaty between the United States (and Canada) and the EU states would be desirable to confirm the importance of U.S.-EU ties. In the aftermath of the Cold War, the symbolic meaning of such a treaty would be no less significant than that of the North Atlantic Treaty after World War II. Signed in April 1999, on the 50th anniversary of the Washington Treaty and on the last year of this century, such a treaty would reaffirm America's commitment to Europe in the combined context of intra-European integration (ever wider) and Euro-Atlantic cooperation (ever deeper). At the earliest possible time, the United States and the EU should also examine and discuss the feasibility of negotiating a Transatlantic Free Trade Agreement. The 50th anniversary of the signing of the Rome Treaties (March 1957) could be the target date for the implementation of such an agreement. Meanwhile, U.S. reluctance to seek a free trade area across the Atlantic while negotiating one such area across the Pacific (as well as in the Western Hemisphere) might convey the wrong message about U.S. interests in Europe relative to its interests elsewhere.

Enlargement of the EU is an important interest of the United States. For central and southeastern Europe, as well as for some of the former Soviet republics (especially the Baltic states), this is a responsibility imposed on the EU states by history as well as by geography. This responsibility must be assumed for the more eligible applicants at the earliest possible time. During the Cold War, U.S. policies gave the states of Western Europe the boost they needed before "Europe" could be launched. After the Cold War, it is the turn of "Europe" to provide a much-needed boost for launching its eastern neighbors toward recovery while NATO enlargement provides for their security needs. Forty years after Europe was conceived in Messina by a small group of states made contiguous by geography and homogenous by history, a European Union of many more states than the current 15 has become not only conceivable, but also desirable.

Except for small states like Cyprus and Malta, such a future will not come quickly, even for the four Visegrad countries in Central Europe (Czech Republic, Hungary, Poland, and Slovakia). The price of enlargement for the EU states (including reform of the Common Agricultural Policy and expansion of the EU structural funds), as well as the political consequences of EU discipline for its aspiring members (even during the multiyear period of transition preceding formal entry), will be substantial at a time when there seems to be little taste for the new math of EU budgeting and EU fiscal rigor. Moreover, significant reforms of Europe's institutions will be needed if the EU is to adjust its governance from the few states that signed the Rome Treaties in 1957 to the geometric maze of two dozen states sometime in the future. The Intergovernmental Conference (IGC) that began in March 1996 may launch some of these reforms, but the century will have long ended before the will and ability to accept and pay the economic and political price of enlargement are mustered. Meanwhile, an unequivocal commitment to launch negotiations for enlargement by a given date, and complete it at the earliest possible time, may have to be sufficient so long as it is sufficiently convincing.

Finally, the implications of EU enlargement on West European Union (WEU) membership (or associated status) and on NATO will demand careful appraisal. For the years to come, states that belong to both organizations will still give precedence to the NATO security guarantees over WEU guarantees. Questions about the U.S. security commitment to NATO members that extend WEU security guarantees to non-NATO states (including new EU members or applicants from Central Europe and even the Baltic states), or to regions of particular significance to some EU members (including North Africa), will, therefore, increase. In other words, EU/WEU enlargement cannot ignore its implications on commitments made by the United States in the Washington Treaty.

☆ POLICY RECOMMENDATIONS

The "new" case for NATO after the Cold War need not come at the expense of the "old" one. In April 1949, the Washington Treaty was signed to avoid the recurrence of the security experiences endured through the previous wars. There was more to these experiences than the Soviet Union and the military threat it raised. Indeed, what was feared most urgently at the time were the political instabilities that delayed economic recovery in states of vital interest to us. In fact, the security alliance between America and Europe came last in the three-part strategy devised by the Truman administration—after, that is, the politics of Marshall aid conditioned economic recovery and the economics of community building permitted political reconciliation.

Entering a new century, the "old" case has to do with the need to consolidate the gains recorded in Western Europe during the Cold War and to protect Europe against new divisions after this most recent war. Not many predictions about the future are likely to withstand the test of time. But at least one will: completing a Europe that is "whole and free" as well as stable and safe will be neither easy nor quick. Accordingly,

- **The United States must continue to play a central role in maintaining the security of Europe.**   Maintaining such a role carries many consequences: (1) as the only available military organization able to perform the tasks of collective defense required by Article V of the Washington Treaty, NATO will remain the body for security for Europe; (2) the credibility of NATO, and that of the United States within NATO, will continue to demand the deployment of a substantial level of combat-ready U.S. land forces in Europe, with a small air-delivered nuclear capability; and (3) the allies will also have to maintain a credible combat force able to support NATO planning contingencies. Otherwise, retention of U.S. forces would prove difficult to sustain politically. Finally, for the WEU to become the European pillar of NATO—while being able to function for EU states outside of Europe—the membership of the Washington Treaty and NATO, NATO and the WEU, and the WEU and EU will have to be coordinated at the earliest possible time.

- **Even as NATO consolidates its existing structures and the commitments of its current members, it must be enlarged to include former Warsaw Pact countries.** Under ideal circumstances, EU and NATO enlargement would be synchronized. But this is not possible. NATO membership for the countries of Central Europe will occur before formal EU membership is achieved. EU membership is less difficult to grant than to adhere to, and NATO membership is easier to assume than to gain. Moreover, the longer NATO enlargement is deferred, the more difficult it may be to enforce, in terms of both Russian resistance and public acceptance within the NATO and EU countries. By the date that NATO membership is extended to those countries in Central Europe whose reforms qualify them to participate as good and reliable allies, the EU must have established a future date certain for full membership of these countries within its ranks.

Among the states that enlargement to Central Europe would leave out, Russia and Ukraine stand out. Whether Russia will ever become a democratic state able to live orderly and in peace with its neighbors is unknown. What is known is that such a happy ending, should it ever happen, will take time. For many years to come, Russia's expressions of geopolitical revisionism will have to be discouraged actively and firmly. It is, after all, a defeated power. But because it is also a Great Power, Russia's political sensitivities, tied to its history, and its security concerns, which flow out of its geography, will also have to be accommodated for many years to come.

Enlarging NATO is a way to manage the former concern. But to do the latter, a treaty (or declaration) of friendship and cooperation between NATO and Russia would recognize the reality of Russia's power, the scope of its interests, and the specificity of its concerns—but it would insist on the need to play by the same agreed rules in all cases, including (and, indeed, especially) rules of consultation for cases about which there would be disagreement.

All kinds of risks to Ukraine's survival exist. Yet, a secure Ukraine guaranteed by NATO and Russia would still Kiev's concerns over Russia and could help usher in an age of reform. It would also create a buffer between an enlarged NATO and Russia. And it would limit apprehensions in Western and Central Europe over the resurgence of Russian influence among the Commonwealth of Independent States (CIS) countries. A secure Ukraine of course would not rule out the establishment by the United States and others—and especially Russia—of close political and economic ties with the government in Kiev.

- **An informal process of transatlantic political coordination will be needed to help address out-of-area, out-of-Europe issues.** Throughout the Cold War, some of the most difficult crises in transatlantic relations occurred outside the NATO area and outside Europe. These crises often reflected genuine differences of interests and traditions between the two sides of the Atlantic. With the Cold War over, more cooperation should be sought, and achieved, than in the past. An informal process that would build on procedures already developed for informal U.S. involvement with the European Political Cooperation (EPC) process would enable the allies to agree on further consultative procedures. These procedures might aim at outlining the first draft of a transatlantic policy in and for areas of converging interest, including the allocation of specific responsibilities and explicit commitments for states directly involved with the issues at hand. For areas or issues especially significant, smaller contact groups should be formed in the context of NATO and pending the further organization of the WEU. These groups could tackle a wide range of issues, including nuclear proliferation, fundamentalism/ terrorism in North Africa and the Middle East, and a strategy for strengthening ties with Eastern Europe, especially the Baltic states.

- **Failure by NATO to meet another challenge after the prolonged debacle in Bosnia would be fatal.** What should have been done in Bosnia, and when, will be debated for years to come. Despite NATO's late but decisive insertion of force under strong and decisive U.S. leadership, no one can forget the sense of outrage and shame felt at the sight of the atrocities that could have been avoided before they started, should have been ended before they escalated, and will now have to be prevented lest they resume. As a result, the public and political mood about NATO has soured and questions about its relevance have shown much exasperation on both sides of the Atlantic.

Whether Bosnia was suited to traditional U.S. peacekeeping techniques, or whether NATO forces should ever again be placed under UN peacekeeping command and control arrangements, are critical questions. The answer, it seems, is negative. Another question is whether peacekeeping in Europe can ever be achieved without U.S. participation in the conflict as well as in the negotiations designed to end it. The experience in the former Yugoslavia suggests not. For lesser conflicts, however, this will be tested by the June 1996 agreement of the NATO ministers that gives European nations greater latitude in conducting military operations without direct U.S. participation.

While NATO will endure in spite of the war in Bosnia, it can also be assumed that it will not be able to outlive many more such episodes. Pretending, as was done in Yugoslavia, that future outbursts of brutality in Eastern Europe are inevitable is a self-serving alibi for doing nothing. What can be learned from the Cold War, however, is that the killing can and does stop when nations and their peoples are provided with enough security to gain the stability they need and the affluence to which they aspire. This, of course, is what the consolidation and revitalization of an enlarged NATO and a wider EU would aim at providing and would help achieve.

☆ CONCLUSION

In contemplating the tasks ahead, it helps to recall that after World War II, organizing the West did not come easily. It helps to remember the criticism that greeted America's vision of the future after Truman suddenly entered the White House in April 1945. It helps to evoke the postwar divisions of U.S. policymakers unable to understand new threats and unwilling to befriend new allies. It helps to bemoan the crises that went unanswered, including the 1948 coup in Czechoslovakia. It helps to marvel at the decisions that were made quickly—proposing the Marshall Plan in 1947, organizing the Berlin airlift in 1948, signing the North Atlantic Treaty in 1949, and intervening in the Korean War in 1950. These memories help because they remind that the "visionary" policies of the postwar years grew haltingly—obstructed by allies that did not always welcome them and by adversaries that did not often accept them.

There is much pessimism about Europe today, as there was 45 years ago when many thought that the worst lay ahead for Europe. But history suggests that such pessimism is unwarranted. Our policy toward Europe remains the most successful foreign policy since the end of World War II. What was achieved during the period is truly extraordinary. In at least half the Continent, nations that used to wage war on each other changed their ways as they enjoyed the benefits of unity—affluence, stability, and security. But continued success in Europe cannot be taken for granted. For the United States to abandon Europe to itself now would be wrong.

The job that the U.S.-led NATO set out to do in Europe 50 years ago is well on its way, but it is only half-done. The time that remains from one century to another, and from one millennium to another, is short. It is, however, likely to be decisive. A time for decisions, it must be a time for leadership.

Russia and the Newly Independent States

Working Group on Russia and the Newly Independent States

Robert Zoellick, *chair**

Keith Bush

Andrew Carpendale

Paula Dobriansky

James Goldgeier

Walter Laqueur

Thomas Navratil

William Odom

Brad Roberts

* *principal author*

Russia and the Newly Independent States

Russia, Ukraine, and the other states of the former Soviet Union are struggling through one of the great transformations of the twentieth century. Frankly, no one knows where the changes will lead.

Some see historical analogies in the fragmentation in recent centuries of the great multinational Eurasian empires, such as the Austro-Hungarian and Ottoman, whose residual conflicts still plague us. But the breakdown and breakup of the Soviet Union was more than the end of an empire. It was also the collapse of a momentous idea, Soviet communism, which had merged one branch of nineteenth-century universalist and "scientific" thought with a reactionary Slavophile movement. So Russians have to cope with more than the dissolution of empire; they also must free themselves from the economic and political wreckage of this failed ideology. The upheaval is so great that even the most basic principles of societal organization are now the subject of daily debate and experimentation.

It is difficult to comprehend how Russians are dealing with this shock. We are not even sure that there is a distinguishing core to which they can retreat. As Count Witte, a turn-of-the-century Czarist reformer explained, "No such thing as Russia exists, there is only the Russian empire." Raised in the belief that they were the privileged people of an exceptional nation, the Russians today suffer humiliation, to say nothing of economic deprivation.

Russians have inherited little to help them face their new political and economic experiment. They have had no democratic experience, no rule of law, no real history of parliaments or separation of powers, no familiarity with property rights, no free press, and no civic society. But they are demonstrating once again the extraordinary Russian ability to endure.

For Russia's diplomatic and defense establishment, the jolt must be even more terrible. Although they recognized the need for change in the 1980s, they had expected to be able to both modernize and retain their great power status. Instead, over only a few years, these proud leaders lost their nation, form of government, economic system, much of their people and territory—all that they had believed in. This took place without any great battle, or even a small one. No conqueror prevailed over their security precautions. It just seemed to happen.

Note: This paper draws in part on ideas set forth in the Trilateral Commission's June 1995 report *Engaging Russia*, by Robert Blackwill, Roderick Braithwaite, and Akihiko Tanaka.

Given this context, one could argue that Russia's recent adjustments and achievements are astounding. Amidst the turmoil, we can identify some signs of reforms taking hold. Individual Russians stand out as people of principle, courage, and commitment to political ideas that most citizens in Western societies take for granted. Others offer vivid testament to the belief that the invisible hand of markets will perform wonders if only it is unleashed. But the chaos has unleashed darker forces as well, in particular a cancer of crime that eats away at legitimate society to a frightening degree.

Although Russia's future is uncertain, we assess its possibilities with respect. Russia is a land of great potential. Its people are highly educated. It enjoys vast natural resources. And Russia has a tradition of rising above calamities of man and nature to exert great influence over Europe and Asia.

☆ ALTERNATIVE SCENARIOS AND RUSSIA'S INTERESTS

We cannot determine, with any reasonable degree of certainty, what will happen within Russia over the rest of this decade. The July 1996 reelection of Boris Yeltsin over a communist provided many in the West with a sense of relief; now, however, Mr. Yeltsin and his government must return to the business of economic reform, fighting crime and social breakdowns, and building a civic society.

For purposes of analysis, however, it is useful to consider three possible scenarios. They are not mutually exclusive.

- **"Muddling through" reforms.**   There is some reasonable probability that Russia could continue to "muddle through" the reform process, eventually developing a relatively stable market economy and democracy. By "muddle through," we mean a series of actions, some of which may seem inconsistent, that eventually produces a satisfactory result. If this transformation occurs, it will take a long time, and the passage will involve many ups and downs.

Most prices are now relatively free in Russia. And the government, including the central bank, at least keeps trying to get inflation under some form of control. While many people are poor, shops are opening, long lines are gone, people are learning how markets work, and property is being transferred (in one way or another) from the state to individuals or groups. Some reports suggest that production has bottomed out, although government statistics are notoriously unreliable.

One could argue that the turmoil reflects the necessary breakdown of the old communist system. Indeed, much of the lost production was for useless, or even counterproductive, purposes in any event. Each day that finds more people with their own personal property, or stake, in the new society, the harder it will be to reverse the changes.

On the political front, a free press, while under threat, seems to be supported by a general audience. Despite setbacks, some reformers still persevere in the central government. Others are trying to create models in cities and regions away from

Moscow. The breakdown of old power structures has created a de facto decentralization of authority, opening the way for greater regionalism within Russia. The Duma functions in a crude fashion. President Yeltsin has amassed significant formal powers, but his idiosyncratic and fitful style of governing still leaves openings for reformers. One of the reformers' hopes is that the military remains divided and would-be authoritarians continue to fail to tap any groundswell of support from a public that seems disillusioned with everyone.

Nevertheless, the rampant crime, the great disparities between the few rich and the great mass of Russians, the collapse of the health care system, even the everyday struggle for survival leaves Russians thoroughly dissatisfied with the reform process. The various reform factions remain deeply divided by differences of personality and recent history. In sum, although political and economic reform might muddle along, it must proceed from a very unsteady base.

- **Continuing weakening of the state and society.** A second possible scenario is that the disintegration of the old Communist and Soviet state will continue, but that neither reformers nor their opponents will prove capable of forging a new system. In this scenario, governments may issue orders and parliaments may pass legislation, but words are not translated into actions. In the absence of the rule of law, individuals and groups are forced to relate to one another through ties of kinship, custom, and power relations.

In this event, the mediating institutions of a civic society fail to take root. Crime becomes even more rampant. Protection societies substitute crudely for law and order. Business may take the form of active trading or barter, with high-risk premiums, but few are willing to invest in an economy where property rights are highly uncertain and time horizons are measured in days, not years.

The military, already deeply split, could lose any of its lingering cohesion and fragment into the modern version of private armies. Nuclear weapons, or plutonium, would become an actively tradeable resource on the world market. This breakdown could lead to a condition of "warlordism" or even forms of civil strife.

The further breakdown of state and society could also lead to territorial fragmentation. Various regions—whether stirred by nationalism, religions, or just a sense they are better off on their own—might quit responding to the central authorities. Other parts of Russia might even assert their independence, as Chechnya did.

A scenario of generalized anarchy would be highly threatening to U.S. interests. The dangers from nuclear and other weapons proliferation are obvious. In addition, internal conflicts, or economic and ecological disasters flowing from them, could trigger immensely disruptive migrations. Weakness might tempt those neighbors eager to seek territories, buffer regimes, or other advantages.

While this scenario is not likely, it cannot be discarded altogether. The continuing chaos, the absence of order, and the threats to the cohesion of Russia itself could motivate Russians to demand a stronger hand and invite leaders eager to exercise it.

- **Authoritarianism: individual and bureaucratic.**   The frustrations of the first scenario, or the fears arising from the second, could prompt an authoritarian response in Russia. Indeed, one can imagine authoritarian efforts to counter both the frustration of a muddling-through reform process and a state and society that are continuing to weaken.

The average Russian lives in fear of mafias and massive shifts in economic forces outside his or her control. Given Russia's authoritarian tradition, a convincing leader could probably gain significant public support, at least for a time. There is no shortage of internal and external enemies against which authoritarians might rally the citizenry. This "strong hand" approach might rely on crude nationalist appeals to build power.

Such an authoritarian political system might be used to continue the implementation of market reforms. Or it might be used to try to preserve the prerogatives of some of the old captains of the command economy. An authoritarian nationalist might also seek to build and expand power at the expense of neighbors and outsiders.

Nevertheless, efforts by individuals to recentralize authority face obstacles. Even the relatively minor conflict in Chechnya demonstrates how hard it is to reimpose Moscow's will over independent groups and regions. No one trusts authorities in Russia. Government only seems able to reassert itself through the imposition of power, perhaps abetted by weaknesses that stem from local quarrels.

Consistent with this lack of legitimate authority, it is likely that various institutions of state control will seek to reextend their reach gradually. They will enhance their assets through crime and corruption. With these assets, organs of the state will seek to make and break leaders who can dispense favors. Rather than aim for total control through one leader, the near-term objectives of these institutional societies will probably be simply to survive and to maintain opportunistic influence for their members come what may.

☆ STRATEGIC IMPLICATIONS

None of these three scenarios, standing alone, has a particularly strong possibility of realization. In coming years, we are most likely to encounter a blurred combination of all three. Moreover, we have little influence over which scenario is likely to come about, although our preference for "muddling through" warrants some effort to shape the future. In any event, the near-term implications for Russia's external policies are basically similar under all three scenarios.

- **Preserving Russia.**   At present and probably for some time, Russia's primary security objective is to preserve the territory of the Russian Federation. As Chechnya demonstrates, Russia has not yet firmly established the residual of the old empire. Russia's political and military leaders are well aware that internal threats, especially if combined with external support, could further dismember their state. Given their recent experience, they will take nothing for granted.

- **Reintegrating the "Near Abroad."**   Second, and close behind, Russians perceive a vital interest in the stability and pro-Russian orientation of the other states of the former Soviet Union. These areas constitute the so-called Near Abroad. In particular, no Russian government will retreat from asserting its interest in the more than 20 million ethnic Russians who live in these states. While Russian policies toward these countries will vary according to circumstances, the immediate national concern is that these neighbors operate in a way conducive to the security and stability of Russia. Russia is already seeking to "reintegrate" them through one means or another. In particular, Russia is pressing to develop and strengthen the institutions of the Commonwealth of Independent States (CIS) in areas such as border controls, air defense, and integrated militaries.

  More specifically, while Russia has acted with restraint towards Ukraine, many Russians see the separation as artificial given the ethnic, historical, and psychological links, and they expect that the pulls of Mother Russia will eventually unite them again. Russia's interests in the Caucasus are motivated by the region's position as a strategic buffer between Iran and Turkey (and Islamic extremism) on the one side and Russia on the other: the mountains to the south approximate one of Russia's few natural land frontiers, and Russia is intent on dominating both sides of this barrier. Moreover, the prospect of great natural resource wealth in the Caspian basin motivates Russia to resecure domination over it. In the states further east, Russia is concerned with protecting ethnic Russians, acquiring natural resources, and warding off Islamic expansion; for now, Russia's policies towards these countries are likely to emphasize containing threats, securing bases for future initiatives, and gaining leverage over resources. Finally, while the Baltics have achieved a special status because of expressions of Western interest, Russians still know these territories as a "window on the sea" they worked for centuries to acquire. Moreover, Latvia and Estonia have large Russian populations, which, in Russian eyes, suffer at the hands of their new countrymen. At a minimum, Russians will expect the Baltic states to take no actions that impinge on Russia's security.

- **Preserving ties with the West.**   Cooperative relations with the West are now a distant third on Russia's priority list. Both the Russian leaders and people are deeply disappointed by what they believe was the West's failure to deliver on its promises of strategic partnership and material support.

  The prevailing view of Russian leaders is that the United States and Western Europe want a one-way street: a Russian retreat in Europe and help in Iraq and elsewhere, without any commensurate sensitivity to Russia's interests or need for respect. In Russian eyes, when Russians sell arms, the West complains that it is destabilizing; when the Western powers ship arms, it is for self-defense and order. Russians perceive that Americans want to stop Russia from building the same type of nuclear plant for Iran that Americans and South Korea will build for North Korea. The West warns Russia not to act too vigorously to counter security risks in the Caucasus, from the Islamic world, and even inside Russia itself, but the West does nothing to help. Until the Russians forced their way into the negotiations among Serbia, Croatia, and Bosnia, Russians perceived no evidence that the West considered their interests. Of course, there are contrary explanations of all these events. And some Russian leaders recognize that generally positive relations with the West are likely to be important for Russia's status and to help achieve future economic well being. But the prospects are wearing thin.

The Russian people believe Western promises have been cynical. They never saw the aid, although they believed it showed up in the hands of the criminals. The foreign economic advisers seemed oblivious to Russia's unique conditions and became enmeshed in Kremlin intrigues. In Russian eyes, Western markets never opened up, except to exploit Russia. For the average Russian, the West never meant to help; some suspect the West actually manipulated Russia to weaken it.

These views often do not stand up to hard factual scrutiny. In reality, the task of overhauling Russia's economic and political systems has been a staggering challenge, and the responsibility for the result has always rested primarily with the Russians themselves. The effect of Western help is dependent on Russian self-help. Nevertheless, many Russians, having started this new age with romanticized expectations, now feel let down by outsiders.

Moreover, the Russian security elite sees the European Union and NATO moving closer to its borders, while still keeping Russia at arms' length. These people view the nations of Central and Eastern Europe not as stable independent states, but as the lands between Germany and Russia, a region of shifting borders, transplanted peoples, and past invasion routes. At a minimum, Russia expects to have a say in this area; it would prefer a sphere of influence.

- **Facing East.** Finally, Russia recognizes, but does not seem overly concerned with, the significance of Asian powers. Immediate demands appear to be crowding out a strategic perspective in Moscow. At present, China faces its own uncertainties, and leaders in Moscow seem to view China primarily as a potential compatriot if the West squeezes the two of them. Relations with Japan are frozen by the impasse over the Northern Territories. The great economic boom of East Asia seems too distant to matter to Russia's present predicament.

- **Russia's agenda.** In sum, for the foreseeable future Russia has its hands full at home and in its immediate neighborhood. Survival has first priority. After Russia returns to strength, it will view its interests coldly, perhaps even resentfully, taking into account Russia's needs at the time. Those needs may include ties with the West; they are certain to include protecting and enhancing the security of a Russian nation that stretches across all of Eurasia, with few natural borders to check perceived enemies or to limit perceived opportunities for influence. In the meantime, Russia will use its place on the UN Security Council, its arms policies, and its looming presence in Europe to demonstrate that Russia cannot be ignored and that Russia's traditional interests should be respected.

☆ U.S. INTERESTS AND GOALS

VITAL INTERESTS

- **The reduction and control of nuclear dangers.**   Although the West no longer faces the mortal threat of an overwhelming nuclear attack from the Soviet Union, we still are menaced by multiple dangers stemming from the old arsenal. Even after full implementation of the major arms control agreements, dismantling programs, purchases of enriched uranium, and ongoing diplomatic pressure, experts estimate that about 12,000 tactical and strategic nuclear weapons will remain within Russia or at sea. The total number of warheads is currently closer to 20,000. In the hands of terrorists, any one of these weapons could kill hundreds of thousands of people.

Some in Russia see its nuclear arsenal as a sign of continuing great power status. This attitude, combined with a mood of resisting the West and cost concerns, has placed the implementation of the START II reductions at risk. One cannot feel comfortable about nuclear command and control in a world where the Russian military is riddled with rivalries and corruption is rampant. The continuing breakdown of order or a move by one faction to secure leverage (or money) would exacerbate the risks.

Russians assert that they are dismantling about 2,000–3,000 warheads annually. (Outsiders appear unable to confirm these statistics, given Russia's ongoing secrecy on this topic.) Unfortunately, dismantlement creates a new set of problems. A terrorist or renegade nation can build a nuclear weapon with about 33 pounds of weapons-grade uranium or 11 pounds of plutonium; there are tons of these materials in Russia. And we already know of captures of groups seeking to smuggle bomb-grade supplies out of Russia.

These nuclear dangers are complemented by the risks of civilian nuclear reactors in the states of the former Soviet Union. Given the poor designs, aging facilities, and likelihood of worker mistakes, another Chernobyl-type disaster is a real possibility.

Finally, the pressure to earn hard currency and to employ nuclear experts has led to sharp differences between Russia and the United States about building nuclear plants in Iran. Enhancing Iran's nuclear capabilities is a definite threat to U.S. and Russian security.

- **The prevention (or limitation) of a militant Russia that threatens European, Asian, or Gulf stability.**   For at least the past three centuries, Russia has been a major participant in European politics and security. Since the late eighteenth century, Russia's acquisition of vast lands in Asia has also made it a force in Asian affairs.

Over the past two centuries, Russian armies have swept across Europe, marching through Paris, Berlin, and a host of other capitals. In turn, a French army occupied Moscow and a German one came within view of the Kremlin's spires. Russia's fleets clashed disastrously with Japan's navy at the opening of this century, but by mid-century Russia's armies had returned to seize the northern islands of Japan.

No country is totally bound by its history. But size and geography cannot be ignored. The fact is that Russia remains a powerful potential force, for good or ill, throughout Europe and Asia.

It would be to our advantage to have Russia as a partner in the twenty-first century. Many of the political and security challenges we face will be found around the rim of Russia, from North Korea to an emerging China, onward through possible conflicts in South Asia and the Islamic world of Central Asia, and on to destabilizing regimes in the Gulf, the Middle East, and the Balkans. If Russia shares our objectives, our likelihood of success will be enhanced.

While Russian support would be important, it is *vital* that Russia not reemerge as a threat to European, East Asian, or Gulf stability. It is in America's geopolitical interest that no nation dominate Europe or East Asia, as the Soviet Union threatened to do. Europe and East Asia are America's primary economic partners. We are also bound to them, especially Europe and Japan, through shared political systems. In sum, Europe and East Asia, in combination with the countries of our own hemisphere, are our probable primary partners no matter what unforeseen challenge awaits us. Russia is the only country that could potentially threaten our partners across both the Atlantic and Pacific.

Russia's policies toward Iran, Iraq, and the other states of the Gulf could also threaten stability and peace in the Middle East, another area of vital interest to the United States and a region easily prone to competition and conflict.

IMPORTANT INTERESTS

• **The establishment of mutually respectful, non-threatening relations between a sovereign, independent Ukraine and Russia.**   Russia's relations with Ukraine are fundamental to the future of European stability. If Ukraine were reabsorbed by Russia, the shock waves would rattle Poland and Germany. Increased German anxieties would affect all of the European Union. If Russia asserted control over Ukraine, Russia's Western neighbors would perceive that the pendulum of history was swinging back, that Russia was reasserting its interests over the lands between it and Germany.

Although most Russians do not accept what they consider to be Ukraine's temporary secession, the Russian government has followed a generally prudent course with Ukraine. Russia has not permitted potential conflicts over the Crimea and the division of the Black Sea fleet to slip out of control.

Some of Russia's restraint may be traceable to its internal problems; it does not have the energy or resources to take on the problems of a Ukraine that has become an economic basket case. At the same time, one major concern has been eliminated. On June 1, 1996, Ukraine sent the last of its 4,400 nuclear warheads to Russia as mandated by the 1994 tripartite Ukraine-United States-Russia accord. Moreover, President Leonid Kuchma's statements seem to point toward a gradual rapprochement between the two countries. The Russian security elite probably assume that the relative disinterest of the United States and the European Union will preclude efforts to integrate Ukraine with the West, opening the way for eventual reintegration with Russia.

It is certainly not clear whether the United States and the Europeans would use force to defend Ukraine against Russia, at least at this point. But Ukraine will probably not face an overt, direct threat in any event. Its greater danger is political and territorial fragmentation after economic collapse. Therefore, the prerequisite for Ukraine's future as an independent state is a successful economic and political reform program. And it is in the strong interest of the United States and Europe that Ukraine's reform efforts succeed.

If it establishes the basis for independence through a sound economy, Ukraine should seek respectful relations with Russia as well as ties to the Western community. Ukraine could demonstrate to Russia that security can be based on mutually beneficial economic ties with a non-threatening neighbor. This relationship would offer Russia a model of bilateral cooperation, as opposed to the model of domination of peripheries through groups like the Commonwealth of Independent States.

- **Russia's development of the rule of law, a market economy, and democracy.** As noted above, we want to prevent Russia from becoming a threat to European and Asian stability. But we also should not ignore the potential benefits of a democratic Russia for the international system; Russia could become a strong partner, following the pattern of Germany and Japan after World War II.

Our ability to affect the course of Russian internal events is, of course, limited. Nevertheless, relatively small amounts of aid to reformers and others seeking to build a civic society could be meaningful.

One dimension of this support is to offer Russia opportunities to participate within transatlantic, European, and global political and economic structures. It is not in our interest to isolate Russia. Economically, Russia has vast potential. Politically, Russia has the ability to impede our pursuit of many other objectives. If Russia decides to isolate itself, that should be because of Russia's choice and actions, not ours.

- **Preservation of the independence of the Baltic states.**   While the Baltic states may not have the same geopolitical weight as Ukraine, they rank high in Western calculations of Russian behavior. Increasingly tied to the West through their own efforts and Scandinavian support, any Russian threat to Baltic independence would disrupt Russia's relations with Europe and the United States

Accordingly, it is also important that the Baltics should seek to develop cooperative relations with Russia, including through the treatment of Russian minorities in accord with the standards of the Organization on Security and Cooperation in Europe (OSCE) and the Council of Europe. The Baltics' best hope for security is a peaceful, democratic Russia that cooperates with the European Union and the United States.

- **Russian respect for the sovereignty of Kazakhstan and the other states of the former Soviet Union.**   The U.S. interests in Ukraine and the Baltic states are worthy of special attention. Yet it is also important that Russia respect the sovereignty of Kazakhstan and the remaining states of the former Soviet Union. In different ways, these states could become a test of whether Russians intend to build a peaceful, democratic nation or to rebuild an empire.

It would be normal for Russia to establish strong economic ties with these countries. These links may even evolve into political frameworks, as they have in Europe. But influence and integration should not translate into domination and absorption.

Although the direct U.S. interest in the survival of these new states may not seem great, small efforts could turn out to be significant both for the countries involved and to signal to Russia what course of interaction is appropriate. In particular, these states' independence could benefit greatly in light of opportunities to transport oil and gas exports through pipelines or water routes outside Russia. The West, in turn, would benefit from diversified access routes for energy supplies.

- **Maintenance of stable relations between Russia and China.**   Russia is weak. China is the rising power in Asia. In the past, such an asymmetry between two large nations bordering one another could lead to tension, even conflict. Frankly, it is surprising that most Russian officials seem relatively inattentive to this potential security problem. Given the size of China's population and the sparse settlement of Russians in the east, Russia might have some anxiety about the future.

It is in the U.S. interest for China and Russia to remain at peace. A conflict between them could be damaging to stability. At the same time, we should be careful about pursuing policies that lead the two to cooperate in challenging Western regimes. We do not want Russia and China to become the leaders of a movement against current efforts to counter the proliferation of weapons of mass destruction, protect the environment, encourage trade and investment, or for other purposes.

BENEFICIAL INTERESTS

- **The prevention of Russian obstructionism of U.S. and Western policies in the UN and elsewhere.**   Russia is not likely to attain the diplomatic reach of the former Soviet Union in world affairs. But Russia still retains considerable ability to obstruct U.S. efforts. As a permanent member of the UN Security Council, Russia still wields considerable influence. Therefore, regardless of developments inside Russia, we should work with Russia to elicit mutual cooperation.

☆ POLICY RECOMMENDATIONS

As the Soviet Union vanished, succeeded in part by a Russia that launched a wave of reforms, many Americans saw great promise in a new Russo-American partnership of democracies. During this phase of relations, the United States succeeded in pressing its interests in Europe, the Gulf, the Middle East, and elsewhere with Russian support or at least acceptance. But over time, certain old Russian behavior has reasserted itself. Now the challenge is to avoid a swing from romanticism to resignation about Russia. What will continue to be needed is realistic engagement.

- **Realistic engagement.**   Russia's future is highly uncertain. While our ability to affect the internal course of events in Russia may be modest, we should not fail to pursue opportunities that appear. Equally important, we should encourage Russia to engage in constructive international behavior. At the same time, we need to prepare for the eventuality that Russia might slip toward authoritarian government and adversarial external policies.

  Whether Russia becomes democratic or authoritarian, we should convey clearly both our steadfast commitment to forwarding our interests and our willingness to cooperate with Russia if it avoids acting in ways that threaten international security and geopolitical stability. Internal Russian political debates should not deter us from pursuing our interests. Not only are we unlikely to influence the course of events inside Russia, but a retreat from pursuit of our interests is likely to trigger miscalculations, both inside and outside Russia, that will result in unintended and unwanted consequences.

  In sum, our policies toward Russia, Ukraine, and the other states of the former Soviet Union must take into account the larger geopolitical context in which we are operating. Russia can be a significant force in both European and Asian affairs. At the same time our dealings with Russia should not be at the expense of the development of other post–Cold War arrangements. While we should reach out to Russia, we should also take steps to ensure against a Russia that is not friendly to us or our allies.

- **Reduced nuclear risks.**   Given the centrality of the nuclear issues to our national interests, this is a top-priority topic for U.S. policy. The Bush and Clinton administrations made significant headway in forging agreements to cut strategic and tactical nuclear weapons and then to help implement these arrangements.

  Early arrangements eliminated between 5,000 and 12,000 Russian tactical nuclear weapons (plus 6,400 American weapons). Once the few nuclear weapons that remain in Belarus have been removed (as they were from Ukraine and Kazakhstan), only one nuclear weapons state will remain following the fragmentation of the Soviet Union. The START I Treaty reduces U.S. and Russian strategic nuclear forces about 40 percent, to approximately 6,000 warheads for each. Once START II is ratified by Russia, each side's arsenal will be cut to no more than 3,500 warheads, a two-thirds reduction from the Cold War highs.

  We have a strong interest in working with Russia to translate these agreements into actual dismantlement and safe provisions for the nuclear materials. Regardless of other developments with Russia, we should support Russian efforts to inventory, safeguard, and eventually dispose of these components. In particular, the United States should affirm and maintain momentum for the Nunn-Lugar initiative. We should overcome bureaucratic impediments to additional purchases of enriched uranium. And we should promptly urge remedies to weaknesses in Russian storage and protection policies.

The theft of highly enriched Russian uranium represents a serious global security threat. It is strongly in our interest to arrange for the transfer of much of that uranium to America for safe storage or manufacture into commercial low-enriched reactor fuel in accordance with agreements already accepted in principle by both countries. Full implemention of these "swords into plowshares" agreements is a serious priority that should be executed expeditiously, using national security as the operative frame of reference rather than commercial considerations.

The United States has taken the lead in projects to address nuclear weapons activities in the former Soviet Union. All G-7, NATO, and EU countries should move this issue to the top of their agendas with Russia. To preserve Russian sensitivities, we should be willing to work through special International Atomic Energy Agency (IAEA) or other multilateral arrangements or to consider reciprocal arrangements.

The United States and the EU have had difficulty coordinating their actions with regard to nuclear power plants in Russia and the former Soviet Union. In part, these problems reflected intra-EU squabbles. Also, reports of German firms interfering with U.S. contracts in Eastern Europe undercut U.S. willingness to finance multi-billion dollar construction projects.

It is not clear that Russia would need its nuclear plants if it moved to market prices for energy and instituted conservation measures. Any solution for the nuclear plants should be in the context of overall energy policies and pricing. In the meantime, the United States and the EU should coordinate to ensure that current operational procedures are as safe as possible and that these rules are applied.

We and our allies also should seek to persuade Russia to avoid any actions that will lead to proliferation of weapons of mass destruction. Indeed, Russia should recognize that the dangers could be great for itself if neighbors, such as Iran, gain nuclear arms.

- **Support for Ukraine's reforms and independence.**   As noted above, Ukraine's success may be the single most important determinant of Russia's peaceful integration into a new, larger Euro-Atlantic community. Therefore, the West should (1) back up Ukrainian self-help policies with tangible support from both the international financial institutions and bilaterally; and (2) convey to Russia that appropriate behavior toward Ukraine is a prerequisite for Russia's economic, political, and security integration with the West.

At the same time, we should explain to Ukrainians that they should not antagonize Russia. Ukrainians, Balts, and others must not assume that the United States will completely bail them out of trouble, especially if it stems from a series of differences with Russia that are subject to reasonable compromises. The solution for

Ukraine, Russia, and the transatlantic nations is for all to treat one another respectfully, in full accord with international norms.

- **Trade and aid for Russia.**   We have already noted our ongoing interest in funding to reduce the nuclear threat. In addition, the United States should devote modest sums to support the development of economic and political reforms and a civil society.

   Russia's transition will take decades, and we are unlikely to be able to sustain large-scale aid for many years. So we should reformulate our aid for longer-term engagement. The larger economic support effort should be financed by the multilateral institutions, which the United States has financed significantly over past years. Small bilateral grants, properly targeted, can go a long way in supporting the development of effective legislatures, a free press, and the development of reform parties. While the returns are uncertain, the gains could prove to be very large.

   Russia's longer-term economic success depends on its effective interconnection with the world economy. Private, not governmental, capital flows are critical. At present, most investors face enormous political, legal, and market risks, so they are hesitant. But Russia has great potential, starting with raw materials, energy supplies, and primary products that can earn foreign exchange. The rest of the world should be sure the door is open for trade so that Russian exporters have a future.

   Our efforts to broaden the outlook of Russian political society should extend beyond the reformist factions to reach the so-called "centrists." These are the groups that may turn out to hold the key to the political balance. We should also engage the Russian military, who are likely to be important in future internal crises or in Russian debates about external policies. We should aim to overcome the military's sense of international isolation and victimization.

- **European security arrangements.**   As discussed in the paper on U.S. international security strategy (appendix E), we support the expansion of NATO and the enlargement of the EU to encompass certain democracies in Central and Eastern Europe. While some Russians will resent NATO's (and possibly the EU's) enlargement, we believe it would be a mistake to let them override our interests in securing a stable, democratic Central and Eastern Europe, increasingly integrated within the transatlantic communities. Indeed, it is important to make clear to Russia, in a non-hostile fashion, that we do not accept that Russia has a right to treat Central and Eastern Europe as its sphere of influence. Nor do we wish to leave Central and Eastern Europe as vulnerable borderlands between Russia and Germany.

   At the same time, we should acknowledge that Russia will have a place in European security affairs, as a matter of fact if not of formal treaty. We should seek to make Russia's involvement cooperative, not challenging. And we should be open-minded about institutional changes to achieve this result.

   Russia seems to have focused on four issues that define its relations with the West. It wants (1) the West to make clear that it does not consider Russia the enemy; (2) new structures so that Russia can participate in the transatlantic community's consideration of security issues; (3) clear expectations on the arms trade that do not leave Russia out; and (4) to avoid NATO deployment patterns (e.g., nuclear weapons, new forces moved eastward) that threaten Russian security.

The U.S. and European governments should suggest creative solutions to address these Russian concerns. Some might be dealt with through a NATO-Russia treaty or charter that is both declarative of intentions and practical in establishing consultative arrangements. Another option is to create new consultative arrangements involving a subset of OSCE nations (perhaps with rotational leadership). In devising these mechanisms for Russia's engagement, we should assume a posture similar to the one we took toward the Soviet Union during German unification: we should promote opportunities for Russia to take part while making it clear that we will proceed in any event. If Russia isolates itself from a cooperative approach toward European security, that result should stem from its own decision, not from our failure to reach out.

We also need to state to Russia, without ambiguity, that our future engagement with it on security matters depends in significant part on Russia's willingness to abide by past treaty commitments. In particular, Russia should not take unilateral action that violates the Conventional Forces in Europe (CFE) agreement.

☆ CONCLUSION

We hope Russia can be a partner of the West in the future. We believe Russia's engagement with, and participation in, regional and global security, economic, and political arrangements would be mutually beneficial. So we want to make sure that opportunity is clearly understood.

At the same time, we recognize that Russia's decisions to participate with us depend heavily on internal developments. Russia must make these choices for itself. We do not serve Russia's interests or our own interests by failing to state clearly what we expect the terms of this engagement to be.

We suggest that we continue to stress our support for Russia's internal reforms, but that we convey that regardless of Russia's form of government we expect its external behavior to conform to certain requirements. These requirements would match the interests that we have noted as most important. They would include support against nuclear proliferation and the acceptance of the independence of Ukraine, the Baltics, and the other Newly Independent States, as well as the nations of Central and Eastern Europe. In assessing Russia's cooperation, however, we should not apply a tougher test to Russia than we apply to our traditional allies.

Appendix D

The Middle East

Working Group on the Middle East

Richard Fairbanks, *chair**

Anthony Cordesman*

Arnaud de Borchgrave

Joseph Montville

Robert Neumann

Peter Rodman*

Stephen Solarz

Dov Zakheim

* *principal authors*

The Middle East

☆ CURRENT ASSESSMENT AND TRENDS

The Middle East is in a race against time. Positive trends—in particular, the most rapid advances toward Arab-Israeli peace in 40 years, which carry with them the possibility of unprecedented regional economic enhancement—struggle against an undertow of negative forces, including rapid population growth, inefficient and wasteful state sectors in the economy, a breakdown of the urban infrastructures and educational systems, declining per capita income and oil wealth, and Islamic extremism. The United States must craft a strategy to ensure that the forces of peaceful progress will be reinforced by successful social and economic development and will outlast, outmaneuver, and overcome the forces of extremism.

POSITIVE TRENDS

If the momentum can be reestablished, the opportunity for an unprecedented peace in the Middle East could become a reality. The earlier combination of the collapse of Soviet power and the coalition victory and political outcome of Desert Storm still tips the balance in favor of the peace process. And in the West's favor, America's Arab allies—especially Egypt and Saudi Arabia—have remained leading forces in intra-Arab politics. Many of America's Arab adversaries either have been deflated by war (Iraq and Iran) or have lost the sources of arms and funds needed to sustain many of their confrontational ambitions. The Palestine Liberation Organization (PLO) has reached an initial peace agreement with Israel and has pressed forward into the Oslo II Accord. Jordan has returned to its more Western orientation and entered into a peace treaty with Israel. The new government of Prime Minister Benjamin Netanyahu, elected in June 1996, has pledged to pursue a different approach to preserving Israel's security than that of the Labor government of Shimon Peres, but has stated its commitment to continuation of the peace process.

Although the peace process is anything but smooth, breakthroughs have been achieved in rapid succession: the Madrid Conference (October 1991); the Oslo Accord between Israel and the PLO (September 1993); the Jordan-Israel Peace Treaty (October 1994); and the Oslo II Accord (September 1995). Hopes were raised and subsequently dashed for a Syrian-Israeli peace agreement. However, several other Arab governments (Morocco, Tunisia, Bahrain, Qatar, Oman) have been exploring the establishment of diplomatic relations with Israel, and many of the Gulf Cooperation Council (GCC) countries have declared their abandonment of the secondary and tertiary economic boycott of Israel.

Despite recent setbacks arising from terrorist attacks against Israeli citizens and the U.S. military in Saudi Arabia, the above diplomatic and political accomplishments offer both the prospect of greatly reducing the chances of another Arab-Israeli conflict and the promise of greater economic cooperation as symbolized especially by the Casablanca conference (October 1994) and the Amman conference (October 1995). The success and longer-term viability of both the evolving peace process and the stability of the entire Middle East depend in no small measure on how the affected populations perceive the improvement in their welfare. Studies by the World Bank and other international institutions reveal that the combination of political turmoil, war, government mismanagement of the economy, and rapid population growth have left development in the Middle East far behind that of Asia and Latin America: in fact, average gross national product (GNP) per capita in the Middle East and the Maghreb contracted by 2.3 percent per year between 1980 and 1992. Rapid expansion of development and economic opportunity is crucial both to the stability of the Gulf and to the constructive resolution of the problems of extremism in the Maghreb.

U.S. global strategy cannot, however, be based simply on encouraging an Arab-Israeli peace settlement and regional military security. The United States must place equal weight on encouraging nations in the region to make sustained economic development their highest priority, to reduce their massive barriers to investment, to privatize, and to ensure that the distribution of income does not simply make the rich richer while failing to reduce the social and economic pressures on most of their populations that act to encourage extremism.

At the same time, U.S. political and military relations with the Arab world have been strengthened both by the progress in resolving the Arab-Israeli conflict (easing one major source of U.S.-Arab tension) and by the victory in Desert Storm, which vindicated those friendly Arab states that chose reliance on the United States as a mainstay of their foreign policy. In addition, there has been a steady improvement since the war in our strategic relations with the southern Gulf states and key allies like Egypt. U.S. military cooperation, especially with Gulf Arab countries, has also improved through additional prepositioning of supplies, access arrangements, joint training and exercises, and arms transfers. Strategic cooperation, strong presence, and power projection capabilities have become critical to regional stability and U.S. global strategy.

NEGATIVE TRENDS

Socioeconomic difficulties afflict many Middle Eastern states. Like Africa and parts of Latin America, much of the Middle East is failing the challenge of development. A stable long-term strategy for dealing with the region must account for and respond to these socioeconomic difficulties and trends.

Failed governments are the principal breeding ground for Islamic extremism. Their resulting flawed policies are a primary threat to our strategic interests. Secular governments and parties have failed to provide both stable patterns of economic development and the infrastructure needed to deal with massive social change. Most Middle Eastern states have not managed their economies wisely, particularly their state and agricultural sectors. Most have also failed to adapt and rationalize government services, and many are corrupt or nepotistic.

Demographics have created a rapidly growing and disproportionately youthful population. Net population growth often exceeds 3 percent annually, and 40 percent of the population of most states are under 15 years of age. This young population often has poor employment and career prospects, with real unemployment rates frequently exceeding 35 percent. These demographic problems generally interact with ethnic and religious problems either because ethnic and religious groups in different countries have different birth rates or because sheer population growth exacerbates ethnic and religious tensions.

Many key Arab states—controlling over 75 percent of the population of the Arab world—have been damaged either by the failure of entrenched socialist regimes or the legacy of such regimes. These states include Algeria, Egypt, Sudan, Syria, Yemen, and to some extent Tunisia and Iraq. Although the oil states of the southern Gulf have avoided the trap of socialism, they have been slow to broaden political participation and have generally failed to create job opportunities for their young and rapidly growing populations. At the same time, weak oil prices, severe cash-flow problems, population pressures, and chronic economic mismanagement have exacerbated internal social tensions in Saudi Arabia and other Gulf states. The more densely populated states such as Egypt and Jordan have also been hurt by the loss of guest-worker income and the dramatic reduction of tourism as the terrorist threats conjure European and American fears.

The most visible result of these problems is **Islamic extremism**. Just as the familiar Nasserite model of "Arab socialism" (of which Saddam Hussein sees himself as the heir) was finally discredited, a new source of radicalism has arisen to fill the ideological vacuum. Islam itself is not a threat either to the peaceful development of the region or to the West. Such threats stem from extremism, hostile and unworkable ideologies, and groups that simply co-opt the name of Islam. Islamic extremism is, however, a political ideology hostile to the West as well as to many Arab governments and is to be distinguished from Islam as a religious faith. Further, it is clearly a key result of socioeconomic problems, but it is certainly not their answer. Islam, like Christianity and Judaism, is not an economic theory or a detailed plan for governing a modern state. A revival of Islam may be an understandable development in light of the failures of secularism, but the extremists who use the name of Islam propose social and economic policies that can only worsen the problems of the region.

Radical Islam cannot solve any of the problems that divide the Middle East and cripple its development. Although this brand of extremism did not spread outward from Tehran after the Iranian Revolution as many had feared, extremist movements have grown in strength in the Sunni-led world since the late 1980s. The fertile soil for their growth has been the deep-seated social and economic frustration of Arab societies still struggling with the dislocations of modernization. But their upsurge outside Iran has also been a function of the seeming loss of legitimacy of

Arab governments whose practical performance and management of the national economy has often been weak and whose moral and political authority has often rested on the secular ideology of the now-discredited "Arab socialism." In many ways the upsurge of Islamic extremism is another by-product of the collapse of the Soviet Union and the failure of Marxism and socialism. This is why some of the Arab monarchies of the Gulf, whose stability was such an object of concern at the time of Desert Storm, seem to be coping better with this Islamic resurgence than the formerly "socialist" leaderships—Algeria, Egypt, and the PLO. The allure of radical Islam is also heavily dependent on a given nation's level of poverty and on the extent of the government's failure to deal with the aspirations of its people.

At the same time radicalism is a regional problem that U.S. global strategy must also deal with. While Islamist extremism is not some centrally directed, conspiratorial "Khomeintern," the contagious effects of extremist movements are not mirages. An Islamist takeover in Algeria would pose a direct danger to the regimes in Tunisia and Morocco, send reverberations through France, Italy, and Spain, and, most important in terms of the U.S. interests in the region, have a shock effect in Egypt. Radical change in Algeria would change the U.S. strategic position in the Middle East for the worse.

Revolutionary Iran continues to pose a strategic problem that combines the drive for Iranian hegemony in the Gulf, opposition to the Arab-Israeli peace process, and a continuing effort to encourage Islamic extremism throughout the region. Although Iran is relatively weak economically and militarily and has lost some of the fervor it possessed at the time of the revolution, it continues to support terrorism, the Hezbollah, and violent anti-Israeli movements such as the Islamic Jihad. Iran is deploying forces designed to threaten the flow of oil through the Gulf and is intimidating its southern Gulf neighbors. In addition, Iran continues to seek nuclear weapons and is building up long-range missile forces as well as its chemical and biological capabilities.

Saddam Hussein's regime in Iraq remains a strategic problem. Iraq possesses a large air force and still has the strongest land forces in the Gulf. The continuing threat Iraq poses to Kuwait was demonstrated as recently as October 1994 and September 1995. Its titular recognition both of Kuwait's status as an independent state and its new border with Kuwait should be seen as an effort to end United Nations sanctions rather than a serious commitment to regional peace. Iraq has repeatedly lied to the UN about its biological, chemical, and nuclear missile programs, and will almost certainly try to maintain a clandestine program to develop and stockpile weapons of mass destruction (WMD). Unless a dramatic change takes place in its leadership, Iraq will most likely act as a revanchist state if UN sanctions are lifted, ready to renew its efforts to secure regional hegemony.

Weapons proliferation and militarism are also regionwide problems. Conventional arms transfers from Russia, China, North Korea, the United States, France, Britain, and elsewhere continue to pour into a volatile region. Some of these transfers to moderate states contribute to regional stability. However, transfers of long-range missiles, long-range strike aircraft, and dual-use nuclear, chemical, and biological warfare technologies to radical regimes are the major problem. These dangers have been exacerbated by the collapse of the Soviet political and economic structure and the resulting risk of illicit transfers of nuclear materials and technology.

The question of Israeli nuclear capability has become a high-profile issue raised by various Arab governments, especially Egypt. It is certain to remain a major issue in bilateral and regional arms control negotiations and in efforts to improve the effectiveness of the Nuclear Non-Proliferation Treaty (NPT). At the same time, Syria's acquisition of long-range missiles and biological and chemical weapons, the threat of proliferation in Iran and Iraq, and trading territories for peace, makes it progressively more difficult for Israel to give up its nuclear capability.

Militarism and the conventional arms race remain a major contributor to social and economic problems, as well as a threat to regional security. While military expenditures have fallen significantly since the Gulf War, they still represent a formidable burden on the region, totaling about $45 billion in 1994 (which equates to consuming 6.5 percent of all annual imports into the region). Algeria is an army with a country, rather than a country with an army; and Morocco is at war with the Polisario. Moreover, Libya, Syria, Iran, and Iraq represent major threats to their neighbors, which, in turn, translates to sizeable military expenditures throughout the region.

The heritage of the Arab-Israeli conflict and the expulsion of Palestinians from the Gulf after 1990 have created other forms of social alienation and economic tensions within the Palestinian movement. There are many Palestinians who are still opposed to peace. This opposition is often linked to Islamic radicalism and has created significant extremist movements such as Hamas and the Islamic Jihad. If the peace process fails, or the economy does not develop, or the secular government fails to meet the needs of its people, these sorts of extremist groups will be a clear and dangerous alternative to the Palestinian National Authority.

Extreme opposition to the peace process among some Israelis also affects the prospects for further negotiations, agreements, and economic development. The assassination earlier this year of Prime Minister Yitzak Rabin by a fellow Israeli illustrates the problem.

Russia's Middle East policy may become more assertive and potentially more destabilizing. Russia's stake in the Middle East, the Transcaucasus, and Central Asia is historically based and geopolitically obvious. Moscow is selling weapons to former clients for needed foreign exchange and nuclear reactors to Iran, as well as cultivating Iraq. It has sought (ineffectually) to develop an independent position in the Arab-Israeli diplomacy. At the same time, Russia also has reason to fear both Islamist radicalism and proliferation in Central Asia and near its southern border.

The Middle East policies of some friendly countries diverge from those of the United States in a number of cases. Few European, southern Gulf, and friendly Asian countries support the United States in its efforts to isolate Iran politically and economically. Several countries, including France, Russia, Qatar, and the United Arab Emirates (UAE), have supported the easing of sanctions on Iraq. Many friendly countries oppose rather than support the U.S. interpretation of dual containment.

☆ U.S. NATIONAL INTERESTS AND GOALS

VITAL INTERESTS

Basic U.S. national interests and goals are not likely to change in the foreseeable future. U.S. global strategy can properly be based on the continuity of current vital and important objectives.

- **Energy security.**   The Middle East has well over 50 percent of the world's known oil and gas reserves. The West will certainly be increasingly dependent on Mideast energy resources well beyond 2020. Energy security is a vital interest, as is ensuring that oil and gas resources remain freely available, without either supply restrictions or massive price swings resulting from regional disruptions or political blackmail. We are becoming steadily more reliant on imports of oil although the percentage of dependence on oil from the Middle East remains much lower than that of Japan or Europe. The United States already imports more than 50 percent of its oil and this dependence may rise to 70 percent by 2020. Regardless of the source of U.S. imports, oil exports are a global commodity, and price increases cannot be geographically contained in a global oil market. As the Carter Doctrine enunciated, no hostile power can be permitted to dominate the Gulf or those resources.

- **Israel.**   Israel is an ally whose security has become a vital interest. In addition to the significant bipartisan political and moral commitment to the survival of the Jewish State, any assault on Israel would be perceived as a threat to the U.S. strategic position.

- **Egypt, Saudi Arabia, and Jordan.**   The pro-U.S. orientation of certain key Arab countries is critical to the our strategic position, as well as to the achievement of U.S. political goals in the region. In this respect, the three aforementioned countries are particularly important. Egypt is a linchpin to stability by virtue of its historical leadership role in the Arab world and its initiation of peace with Israel. In particular, we should continue to work closely with Egypt to help undergird this leadership role. Saudi Arabia has the world's largest oil reserves, is the steward of the two holiest sites in Islam, and is a regional power by virtue of geography and resources. Jordan is playing a pivotal role in the regional security balance now that Israeli-Jordanian relations have normalized and the two countries have signed the Washington Declaration peace accord. An external threat to these countries' pro-U.S. governments would be properly treated as a vital interest. So too would an internal upheaval to precipitate the emergence of governments hostile to the United States. We should be prepared to take immediate action and react promptly with appropriate political or economic assistance.

- **Counterterrorism.**   The West, moderate Arab states, and Israel continue to be the targets of new acts of Middle Eastern terrorism (e.g., attacks on military personnel in Saudi Arabia, the Air France hijacking, the World Trade Center bombing). A more effective, coordinated response—joining together the efforts of the G-7 countries, Russia, and our regional friends—is essential.

IMPORTANT INTERESTS

- **The peace process.**   The Arab-Israeli peace diplomacy continues to be a priority objective because progress toward peace promotes stability in the region and enables us to reconcile our relationships on both sides. Its success reduces the risk of U.S. military involvement in the region and is critical to ensuring that Egypt, Israel, and Jordan continue to act as strategic allies. The peace process also helps to defuse a traditional source of radicalism and anti-American fervor in the Moslem world, although any progress towards peace inevitably incites the most radical and violent elements to oppose this process. The Netanyahu victory reflects a changed political climate in Israel and has slowed the pace of the peace process. What it has not changed is the basic U.S. interest in a successful culmination of the peace process that results in a just and lasting resolution of the major points of disagreement.

- **The energy market.**   The price and supply of energy must not be allowed to be manipulated to the West's detriment by oligopolistic practices or economic blackmail, even if this does not involve major swings in supply and price. The West's policy instruments for countering such a challenge may differ, however, from those that would be used in the case where oil was used as a major weapon—political or economic—or a crisis threatened major reductions in the flow of oil.

- **Gulf security.**   The security of our Arab partners of the Gulf (in addition to Saudi Arabia) is an important interest in light of its indirect impact on Saudi security. An assault on Kuwait or any of the smaller Gulf States would undercut our security position in the region and might well be a prelude to or a step toward a more direct threat to Saudi Arabia and the overall regional balance.

- **The stability of the Maghreb and North Africa.**   Similarly, the states of the Maghreb as well as the Sudan are of indirect importance for U.S. interests because of their impact on our European allies, Egypt's position, and the peace process. We must maintain an interest in Libya's terrorist and extremist actions as well as in the Islamist problem in Algeria and Sudan. The United States must also encourage economic and political reform throughout the region. The European role in the Maghreb is important, first because southern Europe is a major trading partner and energy importer. Also, a sudden flight of exiles to Europe could create major problems for France and other southern European states.

- **Turkey.**   The U.S. link with Turkey, which is an important strategic asset for the West, takes on a new importance because of its potential to become an alternative, pro-Western, secular model of a modernizing Moslem society, especially as it has embarked on a more assertive foreign policy in the Middle East and Central Asia. Turkey, however, faces both serious economic challenges and a growing debate over the role of its Islamic parties in future governments. Furthermore, Turkey's difficulties in dealing with the Kurds internally and transnationally are sources of regional instability. We must recognize and utilize Turkey's strategic importance while helping this key country avoid the pitfalls in its path. We should also encourage political and economic reforms in Turkey and press our European allies to admit Turkey into European organizations such as the European Free Trade Association (EFTA).

- **Political liberalization.**   The United States cannot simply rely on the existing regimes in the Middle East for a long-term, stable global strategy. Culture and religion may alter the form of governmental legitimacy in the Middle Eastern countries, but they do not alter the need for increased popular participation and government structures that reduce the gap between ruler and ruled and allow for more effective forms of pluralism. A simplistic U.S. demand for "democracy" might simply end in putting anti-democratic Islamist forces into power, undercutting our interests, and utterly failing to meet the needs of affected populations. However, a consistent effort to work with friendly governments to encourage appropriate political, liberal evolution can be of cardinal importance in helping to achieve or reinforce the stability and success of secular regimes.

BENEFICIAL INTERESTS

- **Economic reform**.   The United States must look beyond the present emphasis on international payments issues, aid projects, and a generalized emphasis on privatization to find solutions to economic development that show the peoples of the region—particularly the youth—that capitalism and market mechanisms can directly improve their lives and offer hope and opportunities to even the poorest citizens. We must formulate a clear and well-defined strategy to encourage reforms on a regional and country-by-country basis.

☆ POLICY RECOMMENDATIONS

No global strategy can eliminate instability in the Middle East or ensure peace. However, a strategy that recognizes positive trends, identifies key threats, and focuses tightly on key national interests has a high probability of success.

- **The peace process.**   The United States must remain strongly committed to the peace process and must strongly oppose contrary political pressures in Israel, the Palestinian community, and the Arab world. This means opposing threats to halt the transfer of territory for peace, just as it must oppose any tolerance of Islamic terrorism. We must recognize and support the application of UN Resolutions 242 and 338 on all fronts, including Syria. Syria's unwillingness to move beyond arid restatements of formal positions indicates a lack of interest in negotiating a just and lasting peace agreement.

The success of the peace process is critical to many U.S. interests. Its real or perceived failure could lead to the creation of worst case scenarios among many Middle East populations and countries. As a result, intense involvement in the peace process remains a key aspect of U.S. global strategy, as does reinforcing the success of each step in the peace process, supporting it with arms control efforts, and ensuring the success of any future agreements. The U.S. role in organizing economic assistance for the Palestinians and in advancing and nourishing the Israel-Jordan agreement is also vital. The United States continues to be the only party trusted by all sides and is perceived to be the catalyst needed to energize the international community and its institutions.

- **Containment of hostile regional states.**   Iran continues to build up the capability to threaten naval and tanker movements through the Gulf and use its military capabilities to threaten its southern Gulf neighbors. Iran is in the process of acquiring long-range missiles from Korea, and refuelable, long-range Su-24 strike fighters. It also has chemical and biological weapons. Iranian development of fissile material production capability and nuclear weapons could come within the next decade. If Iran obtains weapons grade fissile material from another country, it could build a nuclear weapon in less than two years.

At the same time, the issue of U.S. policy toward Iran remains a matter of controversy with Japan and most of our European and southern Gulf allies, who oppose our policy of containment, advocating instead a "critical dialogue" with Iran. Our policy currently seeks to isolate Iran politically and economically by denying it loans and credits, and placing economic restraints on trade and investment. Our allies support limits on the transfer of arms and some dual-use technologies, but argue that properly structured economic and political relations with Iran will have a moderating influence and keep open lines of communication.

We must firmly support the military containment of Iran as long as the Iranian regime carries out actions hostile to the West, moderate Arab states, or Israel. We must also continue to encourage its European allies—as well as Russia, Japan, and China—to limit or halt all transfers of advanced weapons and dual-use technologies to Iran. The United States should consider careful, targeted third-party trade sanctions on companies or countries that permit such exports, limiting the access of those actors to U.S. markets. Efforts that are too punitive will simply undercut support for the United States and produce a backlash against U.S. policy.

We should, however, make it clear to both Iran and our allies that Iran's government itself holds the keys to ending its political and economic isolation. It is unrealistic for the United States to make political and economic concessions simply in the hope that Iran will change its behavior. We should be open to dialogue with the Iranian regime, in the event that the following criteria for improved political and economic relations are met:

- an end to supporting destabilization and terrorism;
- an end to violent opposition to the Arab-Israeli peace process;
- abandonment of its fervent efforts to obtain and deploy weapons of mass destruction and their means of delivery;
- the peaceful settlement of all oil and gas disputes and regional claims either by arbitration or use of the International Court of Justice; and
- a halt to those aspects of Iran's military build-up that threaten the southern Gulf states and the free flow of oil and trade.

If Iran takes steps to meet the above criteria, the U.S. government should offer the following incentives: a relaxation of opposition to loans and trade; improved political relations; and improved access to international organizations and lending institutions. If hostile Iranian activities continue, the penalties should include heightened U.S. governmental control over trade with American firms, renewed pressure on its other trading partners to restrict commerce with Iran, a heightened U.S. military presence in the Gulf, elevated support for southern Gulf states in countering Iran's military build-up, tighter international controls on dual-use technologies, and a reinforced forward-deployed counter-proliferation policy—including a theater ballistic missile defense capability.

Iraq continues to pose a danger both to its neighbors and to its own population, including the Kurds and marsh Arabs. The Iraqi regime continues to seek weapons of mass destruction and retains (by regional standards) large conventional forces. The United States should seek to maintain the UN effort to rid Iraq, to the greatest extent possible, of its capabilities to build and deliver WMD and should not abandon its efforts to enforce the military containment under any circumstances. The survival of a hostile regime in Baghdad also complicates the longer-term effort to contain Iran, since it renders Iraq an unfit partner for the United States and its moderate Arab friends.

At the same time, pressures have grown in many quarters to lift or ease the UN economic sanctions. In much of the Arab and developing world there is sympathy for the growing economic plight of the Iraqi people and a view that full-scale enforcement of all current sanctions has "failed" since they have not brought Saddam down. The French and Russians have made the case for a relaxation of sanctions in the UN Security Council for economic and geopolitical reasons. These pressures led the United Nations to sign the May 1996 accord (suspended at the time of this writing) that will allow Iraq to export $2 billion worth of oil over a six-month period in order to secure revenue for humanitarian purposes.

We conclude that the United States should make no compromises in maintaining its opposition to all transfers of major weapons systems, new military technologies and production capabilities, and dual-use technologies to Iraq at any point in the foreseeable future. U.S. policy should pursue a strong and unrelenting counter-proliferation strategy that emphasizes the enforcement and strengthening of arms control agreements and controls on technology transfers. At the same time, we believe the United States should abandon the policy of attempting to use a sweeping insistence on enforcing sanctions against Iraq as the primary means to cause the fall of Saddam Hussein and the Ba'th regime. Instead we should continue to insist on a broad interpretation of the requirements set forth in the UN resolutions. We should set clear step-by-step criteria for measuring Iraqi compliance with each major aspect of the UN resolutions and for easing economic sanctions and allowing Iraq to export oil. If Iraq does comply fully with all resolutions, and it uses revenue from the current $2 billion oil export allowance for humanitarian purposes only, the United States should be willing to support further UN offers that would permit Iraq to sell oil. These sales would only be permitted provided that approximately two-thirds of the proceeds are used for food and medical supplies and the remaining third for reparations payments.

In summary, the United States (like other countries) has permanent interests, not permanent allies or enemies. The interest in peace and stability in the Middle East requires us to try to change the behavior of the regimes in Iran and Iraq as well as to examine the possibility of working with those regimes, if and when they change their behavior. We must develop a clearly defined mix of incentives and penalties with regard to Iran and Iraq that both encourages and rewards changes toward more constructive and friendly behavior and penalizes any hostile activities. *A change in relations with either Iran or Iraq, however, must be tied firmly to concrete changes in their policies and to demonstrable supportive action.* There should be no offer of concessions based on hope or the potential power of ephemeral "pragmatists" and "moderates."

- **The Islamist phenomenon.**   The problem of Islamic extremism is the subject of much debate among U.S. experts. One school of thought stresses weaknesses, such as the failure to manage and develop the economy, and the loss of legitimacy of many secular Arab governments. This school creates doubts as to whether the West can effectively resist what has the appearance of a series of mass popular movements spurred by social and economic frustrations. Another school of thought stresses the extremist and anti-democratic nature of some key Islamic political groups and the negative strategic consequences of extremist success in overthrowing governments friendly to us.

Rather than treat the issues of Islam and instability within the Middle East as a "clash of civilizations," U.S. global strategy must focus on both strengthening moderate governments, in particular their ability to manage their economies successfully, and developing diplomatic and economic options that deal with the full range of causes of instability in the region. The United States must avoid strategies based on regional slogans and generalizations and develop country-specific policies that take account of the diversity of national, economic, religious, ethnic, and social problems. The United States should not reject ties to various movements and governments simply because they are Islamic, and we must make clear that dialogue with responsible opposition groups, who pursue positive policies, is a fundamental ingredient of U.S. strategy.

- **Regional cooperation and collaboration with allies in the region.**   The United States must work with important friendly countries and allies such as Egypt, Saudi Arabia, Jordan, Turkey, and Israel to collaborate on mutual problems and to ameliorate their economic and political difficulties. In certain circumstances we can help to foster economic growth and stable political systems that meet domestic imperatives.

The United States needs to take a far more aggressive stand in encouraging economic reform and privatization. Western capitalism has yet to benefit the majority of people in the Middle Eastern states, generally acting only in the interests of a small group of the middle and upper classes. The result is the perceived failure of secular economic alternatives, a perception that has been reinforced by the tendency of the West to focus its aid on large projects and its economic policies on balance of payments and debt issues. This sort of assistance has done little either to benefit the poor or to create an expanding middle class with good career opportunities. The United States, Europe, and Japan, as well as prosperous nations in the region, need to reexamine their own aid plans, their efforts to encourage economic reforms, such as privatization, and the activities of organizations like the World Bank and the International Monetary Fund (IMF) to specifically assist in ameliorating the major causes of instability in the region, and not simply macroeconomic and balance of payments issues.

Economic reform is vital to the success of the Arab-Israeli peace process. Since the October 1994 Casablanca economic summit, prospects for regional economic cooperation (including Israel) have brightened, following the progress in the peace process. Agreement was reached in Casablanca for a Middle East Development Bank and enhanced private sector economic interaction was the theme of the follow-up meeting in Amman.

Further progress is vital, otherwise "grand schemes" and leaps toward economic growth and integration will not be successful. Reform must be primarily national and financed initially from within. Small quiet steps, practical business cooperation, and sound, steady institution-building will be more successful over time than "grand schemes." At the same time, the nations of the region must be made to understand that there will not be a new "Camp David" increase in aid and that further—largely private—investment will only flow toward meaningful economic opportunities that are underpinned by stability.

The United States is uniquely able to foster political evolution and integration, as well as economic growth. In crafting policy in the region, we must continue to understand the forces that affect our allies as we work to ensure regional stability. We must seek approaches to political liberalization that steadily broaden political participation and pluralism without further destablizing fragile governments. This requires a tailored approach to each country, based on quiet dialogue, in which the United States and other Western states encourage a process of change that leads to clear milestones of progress, focusing on the most urgent problems in each country.

At the same time, we must avoid becoming trapped into blindly supporting existing regimes or leaders—particularly governments that fail to move toward greater inclusion in their political processes, meaningful economic reform, and the rule of law. The United States must be prepared for friction with individual regimes and leaders and to take advantage of the fact that the end of the Cold War greatly reduces the risk that such regimes may turn hostile to U.S. policies. An informed strategy must take account of the intelligent and consistent use of time and not treat every problem as a crisis or the excuse for shallow opportunism.

Greater political evolution and collaboration will bring additional regional security cooperation, expanding the security initiatives already underway. The United States should foster *quiet* cooperation in the diplomatic and intelligence fields and take a leading role in NATO's proposed new dialogue with Morocco, Mauritania, Tunisia, Egypt, and Israel. Such efforts would not only underscore the community of interest between the West and moderate states in the Middle East, but would also be of special value as a catalyst for Israel's integration into the Mediterranean security community.

- **Foreign aid.** Although the 104th Congress is reducing the level of U.S. foreign assistance globally, such assistance remains an important tool of our foreign policy in the Middle East. This aid is increasingly concentrated on grant aid to Egypt and Israel and has been crucial to the peace process. Consequently, there is little prospect that the we can make major cuts in such aid in the near term, unless growing economic self-sufficiency in Israel allows appropriate mutually agreed-on reductions in at least the economic components.

The United States needs to re-evaluate the wisdom of the rigid caps it places on its foreign assistance programs. Aid is a powerful and sometimes cost effective tool for advancing U.S. strategic interests in the Middle East. Although our citizens will not support major increases in aid, limited additional amounts to key states such as Bahrain, Jordan, Oman, Tunisia, and Turkey could play a major role in supporting the peace process, strengthening collective defense in the Gulf, checking Islamist extremism, and enhancing U.S. power projection capabilities. Such aid could often take the form of transfers of surplus American military equipment or assistance in military training.

- **Arms limitations.** The proliferation of conventional, nuclear, chemical, and biological arms in the Middle East adds to the dangers inherent in the region's conflicts and poses acute policy dilemmas for the United States. The Madrid multilateral negotiations include a forum on the subject of arms control, which has nurtured an initial dialogue but is unlikely to produce dramatic results.

Since the Gulf War, the United States has continued to supply large quantities of advanced conventional weapons to Israel as well as to its Gulf Arab allies. It has done so primarily for the purpose of strengthening their security, but also to preserve American jobs and the U.S. defense industrial base, and lower unit costs for the U.S.'s own military procurement. However, since 1990, U.S. sales—as well as those of the British, French, Chinese, and Russians—have declined sharply from $20.7 billion in 1992 (in constant 1994 dollars) to $9.4 billion in 1994. At the same time, we have bristled at British, French, Chinese, and Russian efforts to sell arms in the region. Yet conventional arms control remains an elusive concept and the United States can scarcely serve any policy interest by imposing the burden of unilateral disarmament on its own regional allies.

In any case, efforts to limit missiles and chemical, biological, and nuclear arms are a far more critical pursuit, given the fact that the small number of key suppliers have been able to act upon common interests in the past. The states of the Middle East—especially Iran, Iraq, and Libya—are a prime focus of U.S. counterproliferation efforts.

At the same time, Israel's nuclear weapons program remains a difficult political stumbling block. Egypt, in particular, has insisted on some progress in limiting Israel's nuclear program to support the extension of the NPT, and has sought to make proliferation a political issue in the current Arab-Israeli arms control talks. It is unlikely, however, that Israel will accept more than cosmetic restraints on its nuclear freedom of action until the peace process achieves further breakthroughs and until an arms control process is implemented that takes account of the fact that Syria has biological and chemical weapons, and that Iran and Iraq pose potential nuclear, biological, and chemical threats.

The United States must encourage negotiations, joint study, and regional dialogue, despite these problems. We must also continue to encourage efforts to free the Middle East from all weapons of mass destruction. At the same time, there must be a focus on attacking the problem at its source and using every diplomatic tool available to limit the transfer of weapons components and dual-use technologies.

Equally, missile defense—particularly theater-missile defense (TMD)—has become an urgent strategic priority for the United States and its regional allies. The United States should actively pursue its own TMD programs, while coordinating with, and as appropriate, supporting, allied TMD efforts such as Israel's Arrow missile.

- **U.S. defense posture.**   Current U.S. military strategy calls for forces that can fight two near-simultaneous major regional contingencies. The real issue, however, is the future ability of the United States to intervene in one major mid- or high-intensity conflict in either the Middle East or Asia, and how the impact of ongoing reductions in U.S. forces will erode the military's power projection capabilities and overseas presence. U.S. power projection capabilities are of critical importance to the security and stability of the Middle East, and there are still serious near- and long-term risks that the United States will face military contingencies in this theater.

Although the success of Desert Storm reestablished the credibility of American resolve, power, and deterrence, the memory of a past victory is a wasting asset. The weakening of the overall U.S. defense posture in Europe and the continental United States (CONUS) since Desert Storm requires a serious reassessment of how to provide the mix of regional presence, prepositioning of equipment, and power projection capability necessary to deal with regional threats and keep the credibility of its deterrent. It also requires much better defined goals for building up the military capabilities of the southern Gulf States, providing military aid to Egypt and Israel, and developing effective regional counterproliferation capabilities.

The United States may be the world's only remaining superpower, but it is steadily losing its ability to act unilaterally without powerful regional coalitions. We must not only retain powerful military capabilities to deter and, if necessary, defeat states like Iran and Iraq; we must also build a mix of long-term cooperative security arrangements based on (a) bilateral security agreements with key allies including Bahrain, Egypt, Israel, Kuwait, Qatar, Oman, Saudi Arabia, Turkey, the UAE, and possibly Jordan; (b) informal arrangements with the GCC and contingency planning with European allies, particularly Britain and France; and (c) out-of-area planning within NATO.

The United States should back such agreements with efforts to advance regional arms control and international agreements that prevent or limit the rate of proliferation of weapons of mass destruction. Efforts should also be taken to develop a successor to the Coordinating Committee on Multilateral Export Controls (COCOM) that will limit arms transfers to radical states such as Iran, Iraq, and Libya. The United States must support movement towards peace, cope with the risks of proliferation, and confront potential aggressors with the reality that any use of intimidation or force will be met with defeat. We must also now accelerate the buildup of power projection forces with strong counterproliferation capabilities, including theater missile defense, capable of providing a new form of extended deterrence against rogue states with the ability to employ theater nuclear weapons.

International Security Strategy for the Post–Cold War Era

Working Group on International Security

Robert Murray, *chair**
Harold Brown
Arnaud de Borchgrave
Fred Iklé
Edward Luttwak
Dave McCurdy
Brad Roberts
John Rogers
Don Snider

* principal author

International Security Strategy for the Post–Cold War Era

☆ CURRENT TRENDS

The collapse of the Soviet empire brings fundamental change to the international security system. A half-century of war and near-war for the United States and its allies is over, and the only hostile counterweight to the military power of the United States is gone. Left behind is a weak Russia struggling to define a new political and economic system and a Russian military uncertain about its purpose and its future. Russia's neighbors are impelled to assert more independent futures for themselves. Central European states are inspired to reassert their westward natures in political and economic philosophy and policy and to strive to be included in Western security arrangements. Certain governments—North Korea, Syria, Iraq, Cuba—are left without the psychological and practical support they need to pursue policies of confrontation, even though they retain dictatorial power. Questions of internal legitimacy arise for remaining Communist governments, particularly China, Vietnam, and Cuba. China's growing economic and strategic weight will make her of rising importance in the next century. In the Middle East, Saddam Hussein discovered that the Soviet collapse facilitated his rebuff, not his aggression, and progress toward an eventual Arab-Israeli peace has already fostered unprecedented economic cooperation in the region. In the former Yugoslavia, on the other hand, ancient enmities and ambitions have been renewed, creating an international moral dilemma and the long-range possibility of a wider European conflict. In many parts of Africa, questions of political legitimacy and economic viability abound, raising many issues for the international community, including issues of military intervention. Thus, the fall of the Soviet empire opens a period of profound change and considerable uncertainty for the United States and for many other nations.

But the end of the Soviet empire is not the only source of significant change in the international system. Far-reaching changes in international economics are occurring due to continuing advances in technology and growing economic interdependence among nations. Nations are recognizing that decentralized, market-oriented economies produce faster economic growth, and consequently make possible modernization and a higher standard of living. These economic changes are moving nations toward market economies and liberal democracy and away from more centralized economies and authoritarian political systems. These political and economic changes tend to advance the incentives for peace over war among nations with a substantial stake in the international system.

Most countries are part of the international system, follow its rules, and want the stability that enables the system to function. There remain, however, nations whose stake in the international system is less. Iraq and Iran are examples. Both Iraq and Iran could benefit in practical ways from a more cooperative approach to international relations, but neither pursues such a course for reasons, perhaps, of internal political control and ideology. There are also many countries that, as a practical matter, are largely outside the international system: confrontation states (North Korea, Syria, and Cuba), many countries in Africa, and some countries in Asia. Many of these states have endemic cultural, political, economic, health, and environmental problems, which are already having international repercussions. Some states—those with a high rate of population growth, high percentage of unemployed young people, and poor economic prospects—face a bleak future and are likely to be a source of friction in the international system. Several states have the potential to pose great danger to their neighbors and to the international community by developing nuclear or biological weapons. All together, these states and peoples will reflect needs and present challenges that will be hard for the international system to ignore.

There are also a number of non-state actors outside the international system but aiming to influence it. This is not a new circumstance; what is new is that these political actors no longer have Soviet support for their activities. In poor countries, political actors with only revolutionary routes to power available to them are using the obvious disadvantage and disaffection of people to mobilize political support for revolution. They do this by promoting hatred and creating enemies, often including hatred of the United States. Lacking practical remedies to the real problems of poor states and peoples, these revolutionary leaders promote terrorism and instability. This is particularly manifest in the philosophies and actions of a number of militant Islamists.

Revolutionary ideology and violent leaders are not confined to poor countries. In the United States, the Oklahoma bombing of a federal building and the growth of militias suggest a homegrown security problem for us, and the New York Trade Center bombing suggests a domestic vulnerability to violence by international actors. In Japan, the Aum Supreme Truth cult demonstrated the vulnerability of Japanese society and, by implication, the vulnerability of other societies. According to Senator Sam Nunn, who studied the cult's activities following the Sarin gas attack on Tokyo's subway, the cult was a doomsday-type cult that was projecting Armageddon between Japan and the United States. The cult, with a reported 10,000 followers in Japan and 30,000 in eastern Russia, possessed (and used) nerve gas and was attempting to acquire nuclear and biological weapons and to recruit Russian experts in these fields to assist in the overthrow of the Japanese government. As Senator Nunn observed, "We . . . have a real vulnerability . . . when groups like this, that are willing to do the unthinkable, are also able to get unthinkable destructive power in their hands."

Another class of non-state actors is having a growing effect on the international system: international criminals profiting from the worldwide demand for narcotics and from the opportunities for corrupt personal gain present in the fluid political circumstances of many countries in the post–Cold War environment. The increasingly international character of certain kinds of criminal behavior is facilitated by the growth in computing and communications technology, and the impact on our security and well-being shows no sign of lessening.

Finally, there are powerful states not yet full members of the international system who will have a crucial impact on that system in the next century. Russia and China are the most prominent of these states. The future direction of both China and Russia is uncertain. Both have the long-term potential to be leading, constructive participants in the international system. Alternatively, both have the potential to challenge the international system and the United States in powerful ways, including militarily. It is obviously in our interest to help bring China and Russia into the international system as full partners with full obligations and benefits, but we have not yet devised the policies or mobilized the resources and energies of the West sufficiently to assure success in this endeavor.

☆ U.S. SECURITY INTERESTS

We are in a period of transition. The Cold War is over and there are now no worldwide confrontations or opposing blocs. In this transition, we should look particularly to our long-term interests to guide our security policies. We have enduring security interests ranging from vital to beneficial.

VITAL SECURITY INTERESTS

- **Preventing direct threats to our homeland.**   This interest is likely to sharpen in the coming century as new technology creates new risks. The most potent threat to the United States in the twentieth century was the threat of deliberate attack by the Soviet Union with intercontinental nuclear-armed missiles; that threat has now dissolved, although a weak and inchoate Russia still maintains a huge nuclear arsenal. In the next century, nuclear-armed missiles of Russia and China, and perhaps of other states, would pose grave dangers to us if those states were hostile to the United States. Moreover, there may be weapons in addition to intercontinental missiles that present dangers to the U.S. homeland, particularly nuclear and biological weapons delivered by means other than intercontinental missiles. There are also various forms of international terrorism that could pose dangers for us. More speculatively, there are possibilities of attack on our financial and other systems whose core features depend increasingly on computers and communications and that may therefore be susceptible to interference, and possibly manipulation, by an adversary.

- **Assuring that hostile powers do not dominate key places and key components in the international system.**   The United States has been concerned for much of this century that Europe, the Middle East, and Asia not be dominated by hostile powers and that essential economic resources not be controlled by such powers. We have many times risked and several times engaged in war to prevent such occurrences. We still maintain large standing military forces around the world in part for this purpose. This will continue to be a vital interest of ours in the next century.

- **Ensuring the stability of, and U.S. access to, the international system.**   We have a vital interest in the stability of the international system and in assuring economic, political, and military access for the United States and for individual Americans to the nations and commerce of the world. American leadership helped create the international network of economic, political, diplomatic, and security relationships and institutions that made it possible to achieve significant stability and progress in the second half of this century. The welfare of the United States and most other countries depends on the continued health of the evolving international system. It is in our interest to continue striving for an open, inclusive international system in all its dimensions and to maintain the stability of that system.

IMPORTANT SECURITY INTERESTS

There are also security interests of the United States that are particularly important although perhaps not absolutely essential to the existence or nature of American society. Among our important security interests are

- **Maintaining intact NATO and the U.S.-Japan bilateral security relationship.** The North Atlantic Treaty Organization, including its military components, and our bilateral security relationship with Japan are the principal foundation blocks for American security policy and for advancing our vital interests in conjunction with our allies. The U.S.-Japan security relationship is central to American security interests in Asia, and NATO is the vehicle for assuring collective security in Western Europe and for building a wider security arrangement for all Europe. Also, the NATO military organization is the most practical multilateral vehicle for military action in places that, like Bosnia, threaten international order. Maintaining healthy security relationships in Europe and with Japan will remain key interests of the United States in the next century.

- **Promoting regional stability.**   While we should acknowledge the primacy of regional states in most regional affairs, we have a stake in regional affairs that have implications for the international system and for friendly nations. We have worked with other countries and within the United Nations to resolve regional disputes peacefully. We have acted to ensure the survival and well-being of friendly governments, to prevent the domination and control of particular regions and important resources, and to reduce the possibility that nuclear weapons would be used in regional disputes. We have encouraged leading states to adopt constructive policies toward regional issues. Assuring regional stability will remain an important interest of the United States in the twenty-first century.

- **Supporting human development.**   Many states face formidable problems in meeting even the basic human needs of their populations, and for many states this situation is likely to become worse, in some cases beyond the ability of local governments to cope. Country problems that cannot be solved within the country will become problems for the international community. Thus it is an important interest of ours to help promote the economic and political development of underdeveloped, troubled nations while there is the opportunity for constructive local solutions, before they become international crises.

- **Advancing human rights.**   Human rights are now an international as well as national matter in the U.S. view and in the view of other governments. The atrocities in the twentieth century, although not original, have been of nearly unimaginable scale and ferocity. They have awakened many people and governments to the view that such behavior—indeed, any behavior indicating that individual human rights are systematically abused by governments—is intolerable, and that governments practicing such behavior pose a threat to international civilization as well as to their citizens. This attitude is reinforced by modern communications technology—the CNN factor—which makes the political conditions of nations, including their human rights abuses, more transparent than in earlier eras. The UN Charter speaks to the importance of human rights and the responsibility of governments toward their people. More recently, the 1975 Final Act of the Helsinki Conference on Security and Cooperation in Europe codified the international significance of human rights. The Final Act agreement requires signatory nations to respect human rights and fundamental freedoms, including the freedom of thought, conscience, religion, or belief for all without distinction as to race, sex, language, or religion and to promote and encourage the effective exercise of civil, political, economic, social, cultural, and other rights and freedoms all of which derive from the inherent dignity of the human person and are essential for his free and full development. The signatory nations to the Helsinki Final Act are by no means a majority of the world's nations, yet they represent an important and increasingly influential world view. The United States is one of the signatory nations. We have a legal, as well as a moral and practical, interest in protecting and advancing human rights.

- **Advancing the common security interests of friendly states in multilateral and bilateral associations.** This should include support for a strengthened role for the United Nations in peacekeeping and peace-enforcing in regional disputes. It is also in our interest that NATO countries continue to cooperate militarily and to maintain interoperability of military doctrine and equipment and training, so that those countries that are willing can form effective coalitions for specific peace enforcement and other military operations, such as for the Gulf War and for Bosnia. Finally, it is in our interest to promote and participate in regional associations that encourage peaceful resolution of disputes and to work with nations bilaterally toward that same end.

BENEFICIAL SECURITY INTERESTS

In the category of "beneficial" interests is that of encouraging military-to-military relationships, as well as other forms of cooperation, between the United States and other states. We should do so on a bilateral and multilateral basis, in order to provide a practical basis for coalition military operations when it is in our interest to engage in same.

☆ U.S. SECURITY POLICIES AND RECOMMENDATIONS

There is no substitute for American engagement and leadership on the principal international security issues. The United States is well positioned for the task. We approach the twenty-first century with established democratic political ideals, the strongest economy, the most powerful armed forces, and the principal leadership position in the world. Remarkably, perhaps, the U.S. leadership role is not only acknowledged but often welcomed by other nations; and American armed forces and defense spending, although disproportionately greater than that of many other nations combined, have not inspired a countervailing arms race. On the contrary, American power appears, so far, to have both discouraged such an arms race and helped provide the secure world framework that makes it unnecessary.

NATO remains the centerpiece of U.S. security policy in Europe. But in Europe, we have yet to reconcile our declared intention of ultimately expanding NATO's treaty obligations to Central European states with our ambition to integrate Russia into the international community. In Asia, we have yet to feel the impact of post–Cold War political circumstances on our security alliance with Japan. Can the U.S.-Japanese security relationship continue intact over the next quarter-century? It is in our interest to help make the answer, "Yes." It is also in our interest that China be integrated into the international community. In the Middle East, it is an important interest of ours that the peace process between Israel and her Arab neighbors be fully successful, and we should be prepared to help ensure that the security promises made in peace treaties endure. We should also be prepared to continue a policy of isolation and containment of those few states that persist in hostile policies toward the United States.

The United States is potentially disadvantaged in world leadership in the next century by unresolved domestic problems and by an already staggering debt that continues to grow through annual budget deficits. One consequence of these domestic political and financial concerns is pressure to reduce funding for programs that support our national security interests.

A particular example of reduced funding for such programs is the funding for the foreign assistance program. It is recommended in the global problems and opportunities section of this report (appendix G) that it should be U.S. policy to improve the effectiveness of our foreign assistance program in support of humanitarian needs, longer-term economic development, and democratization. We endorse that recommendation. We also urge additional foreign assistance in support of more rapid dismantling of nuclear weapons in the former Soviet Union, as outlined in the Russia/NIS section (appendix C). Nuclear weapons remain the most potent threat to the American homeland; helping destroy these weapons is a singularly cost-effective security investment.

An important element of future American leadership on security matters will continue to be our willingness and ability to maintain forward-deployed armed forces in key areas and to use those forces in a manner that strengthens deterrence, contributes to resolving conflicts, and builds military-to-military relationships with regional states. The size of our armed forces and the magnitude of our military deployments are properly shrinking. But forward deployments of our armed forces continue to be essential for American security purposes.

American security policy in the next century should strive to accomplish the following:

- **Preserve old alliances and avoid new enemies.**   The North Atlantic Treaty created an organization that has become history's most cohesive and successful political-military alliance. The North Atlantic Treaty Organization began as, and remains, a defensive alliance. The NATO allies have maintained an unswerving commitment to the defense of each other generally, and to the defense of Europe particularly, for nearly a half-century. The alliance is robust and flexible enough to accommodate the occasionally divergent political views of its members. Member nations have built highly professional, cooperative military forces in support of the alliance, and its integrated command and staff is unique. It has proved the most effectual vehicle for cooperative military action in Europe. It has demonstrated that it can cooperate with the United Nations and with other political-security structures in Europe. NATO is an appropriate base on which to build expanded security arrangements with the states of Eastern and Central Europe, including Russia. Expanding NATO in a way that strengthens security throughout Europe, promotes Russian cooperation rather than a fearful reaction, keeps the United States as an anchor in European defense, and avoids drawing the United States into commitments it is unable to fulfill, are the challenges for the policies of the United States and other NATO members in the coming decades.

  The alliance with Japan is as important for our security interests in Asia as the NATO alliance is in Europe. U.S. security policy should aim at a U.S.-Japanese partnership for the post–Cold War era that strengthens the prospects for peace in Asia and that helps bring China into the international community as a full member. Neither the United States nor Japan should allow policies of confrontation on matters such as trade to jeopardize our larger, common interest in a stronger and closer partnership on Asian security matters and on promoting the stability and well-being of the international system in which we both have a vital stake.

Also in Asia, the U.S. security alliance with Korea will remain essential as long as North Korea pursues a confrontation policy, if we are to avoid renewed war on the Korean Peninsula. If Korea reunites peacefully and continues as a democratic, free-market nation, we should seek to develop a broader security arrangement for Asia that includes the United States, Japan, China, Russia, and the unified Koreas. Until then, a standing security dialogue involving these same countries would be highly desirable, including North Korea if that country is willing to participate. In Southeast Asia, reinforcement of the broader security deliberations of the ASEAN Regional Forum will help strengthen stability in that region.

- **Prevent the proliferation of nuclear, biological, and chemical weapons and technology.**   What had been until this century a very modest advance in technology has become an advance so swift and comprehensive as to redefine the character of our planet. Many of these developments have raised our standard of living, but some pose great threats. Weapons of mass destruction are, obviously, in the latter category.

Most nations recognize the dangers of such weapons and have agreed to various limitations on their actions with respect to them; among the remaining countries, the countries that evoke proliferation concern are few in number. There is no inevitable trend toward the broader diffusion of nuclear, chemical, and biological weapons. The effort to prevent proliferation thus remains a sound and important priority of American security policy.

International treaties exist or are pending with respect to the known types of weapons of mass destruction: nuclear, biological, and chemical. Chemical weapons were the first to be banned, a result of the experience of World War I, in which over 1 million casualties and 100,000 deaths resulted from chemical weapons use. The Geneva Protocol of 1925, which the United States ratified in 1975, prohibits "the use in war of asphyxiating, poisonous or other gases, and of all analogous liquids, materials or devices . . . (and) the use of bacteriological methods of warfare. . . ."

A ban on biological weapons was negotiated in 1972, when the United States et al. signed, and later ratified, the Convention on the Prohibition of the Development, Production and Stockpiling of Bacteriological (Biological) and Toxin Weapons and on Their Destruction. The Convention binds the parties not to develop, produce, stockpile, or acquire biological agents or toxins (except for peaceful purposes) or weapons and means for their delivery; and it requires that all such material be destroyed.

The Treaty on the Non-Proliferation of Nuclear Weapons (NPT) was signed in 1968 and was ratified by the United States in 1969. The treaty is meant to prevent the spread of nuclear weapons, to ensure that peaceful nuclear activities are not diverted to making weapons, to cooperate in the peaceful uses of nuclear technology, and to promote comprehensive arms control and nuclear disarmament. The treaty provides for safeguards against cheating, including rights of inspection (and in this respect goes farther than either the chemical or biological arms control agreements, both of which are deficient in terms of safeguards). It was agreed in 1995 by signatory countries to extend the treaty indefinitely, an accomplishment attributable in part to strong U.S. leadership.

These treaties have various deficiencies as guarantors against proliferation. Despite their deficiencies, and in order to correct their deficiencies and advance their purposes, these global treaty regimes for the control of nuclear, biological, and chemical weapons and the more modest regime of missile technology control merit increasing prominence in the post–Cold War era. While these regimes are not panaceas, they are useful in constraining proliferation and in limiting its dimensions. Moreover, there is no substitute for a legal framework that embodies political norms related to such weapons; among other things, such norms help generate the political agreement needed to pose threatening reaction to instances of egregious behavior by a state.

These treaties will not be viable without strong, continuing American leadership—leadership of the kind shown in recent negotiations to win the indefinite extension of the NPT. The nuclear nonproliferation regime requires U.S. leadership to strengthen the International Atomic Energy Agency and to implement the various undertakings agreed at the May 1995 NPT extension conference. Determined leadership is also needed to halt biological weapons proliferation and to add compliance provisions to the Biological and Toxin Weapons Convention, which is presently without such provisions. The success of these several regimes will require U.S. leadership in defending the norms embodied in these treaties, as well as high-level attention to their implementing arrangements. Each regime requires detailed export control systems in each government to make them effective, and each regime must deal with acknowledged proliferation problems in Iraq, North Korea, and (for biological weapons) Russia. Finally, there appears to be a need for better political-military planning for action against potential proliferators, in the event military action is judged appropriate.

- **Ensure a peacemaking capability in the national security establishment.** The Cold War's end relieved the advanced countries of the risk of interstate war among themselves. It did not relieve other countries, mostly Third World countries, of the risk of internal or regional conflict. Nor did it relieve the advanced countries of all interest in the outcome of these Third World conflicts or of the expressed need to intervene periodically to influence their outcome.

Most interventions in nations in crisis do not involve military force, and many interventions occur through multilateral agencies. They involve UN agencies such as the High Commissioner for Refugees, other multilateral organizations such as the international development banks, voluntary relief agencies such as the Red Cross, and various assistance agencies of national governments, such as the Agency for International Development in the United States. But periodically outside military force is used in local crises. When military force is used, the political stakes for the intervening nation are greatly increased. The United States has intervened with military force on a number of occasions, both during and since the Cold War.

Outside military intervention in local conflicts is usually for peacekeeping or peacemaking purposes. *Peacekeeping* means using military personnel to observe the implementation of a cease-fire or peace agreement by the parties to the agreement. Although danger is not unknown in peacekeeping missions, they are intended to be essentially benign missions, predicated on a sufficient consensus among the conflicting parties to enable peacekeeping soldiers to carry out their duty as neutral overseers and referees of the terms of the agreement. American military peacekeepers in the Sinai desert, for example, have monitored the peace agreement between Egypt and Israel since 1979, providing assurance to both states that the terms of the agreement are being complied with. If the consensus for peace between the parties were to break down, however, then it would no longer be feasible for the outside peacekeepers to play their peacekeeping role. This happened in the Sinai in 1967 under an earlier peacekeeping agreement involving United Nations peacekeepers. When the consensus breaks down, the peacekeepers either withdraw, as they did (prematurely) in the Sinai in 1967, or they continue in place but become ineffective, as has happened frequently to UN peacekeepers in Lebanon.

Peacemaking is a more dangerous job. *Peacemaking*, or peace enforcement, means undertaking the task of halting a conflict or of enforcing a peace or cease-fire agreement. Peacemaking requires a greater political commitment on the part of intervening states; it carries with it the assumption of danger for the forces involved; and it ought to include the expectation that casualties may occur in the intervening force.

The United States has considerable experience with peacemaking missions, some successful, some unsuccessful, and we can learn from those experiences. Here are examples:

- We intervened twice in Lebanon between 1982 and 1984. The first, brief intervention in summer 1982 was to enable the Palestine Liberation Organization (PLO) to withdraw its combatants from Lebanon following the Israeli invasion of Lebanon earlier that summer. A small U.S. Marine force was positioned between the conflicting PLO and Israeli forces, enabling the PLO to withdraw in safety. The political objective was limited, the military mission clear, and the intervention succeeded.

- The second Lebanon intervention failed. This intervention began in September 1982, shortly after the first success, and continued to February 1984. The political objectives of the second intervention were vastly more ambitious: to facilitate the swift withdrawal of all Israeli and Syrian military forces from Lebanon and to encourage the several Lebanese factions to halt their civil war. The military force inserted was multilateral: American, British, French, and Italian—but each unit was under its own national command. The role assigned the U.S. military in supporting the political objectives was changed several times in the ensuing months, was always poorly understood, was hampered by poor and sometimes conflicting communications between political and military authorities, and in the end was unsuccessful. In less than 18 months, the United States abandoned its political objectives and withdrew its forces after losing over 250 American military and civilian lives. (The lives of many French soldiers were also lost.)

- A decade later, a similar set of U.S. military interventions was ordered by the president with similar results, this time in Somalia. By 1992, political authority in Somalia had fragmented, fighting among Somali clans was common, and mass starvation was occurring. The president ordered the U.S. forces to intervene for humanitarian reasons—to prevent further starvation. The U.S. force, in coordination with a Special Ambassador, a person of great experience in Somalia, and in cooperation with relief agencies, created a security and logistic environment that allowed the starving to be fed. This intervention succeeded.

- The second intervention in Somalia, following immediately upon the first success, was under United Nations authority and command. The United States was an active political participant, however, and a provider of troops to the UN force, and the senior UN official on the ground was an American. The political objectives of this second intervention were much broader than the first, and the coalition military force was weaker and lacked certainty of purpose and unity of command. The intervention failed, and the UN force had to be withdrawn.

From these and other experiences we learn the importance of having realistic political objectives, based on intimate knowledge of the local situation and a clear vision of what feasibly can be achieved; congruent military objectives, including clear rules of engagement and unity of command for the military force to enable sound execution of the mission; a clear understanding among the principal participants of the role each will play, and then continual, open communications among the principals, both in the field and in Washington; and political and military leaders on the ground who are highly experienced, highly knowledgeable of the local situation and local leaders, and who work cooperatively with one another and with Washington in adjusting policy and performance to meet the dynamic local situation as it unfolds.

Interventions in Third World conflicts such as in Lebanon or Somalia or Haiti or Bosnia will always be politically difficult for the president. Such interventions are seldom seen by Congress as central to American interests, and the president is often required to spend more political energy in gaining congressional support and more time in trying to assure success of the endeavor than he would like. Interventions are usually risky ventures too, because of the lack of deep political support—bad judgment, poor leadership, bad management, or bad luck at any key point will deliver a political failure, and failure as well as success has both domestic and international implications, as Lyndon Johnson, Jimmy Carter, and Ronald Reagan learned.

Nevertheless, presidents will accept the risks when they see the need for intervention. The national security establishment needs to prepare in advance, in anticipation of such a decision, and by and large it does. The military in particular are increasingly well-prepared. The armed forces today are composed of intelligent, disciplined, motivated, well-led, well-equipped, well-trained people. The armed forces today are at an historically high level of capability and readiness. Military leaders engage in extensive planning and military exercises to better understand and prepare for intervention missions. There are now a number of highly experienced military leaders who have led and participated in such missions. Greater emphasis on education and training for intervention should be a more important part, however, of the curriculum in military schools and war colleges.

Military intervention, however, is not primarily a military problem. It is a political problem of the most sensitive kind. When military force is used, the political stakes increase greatly. Success in intervention missions requires, among other things, the most careful selection of realistic objectives by the National Security Council (NSC) and the president. It requires the Cabinet secretaries to select the most promising leaders for the mission, diplomatic and military. It requires the NSC to assign responsibilities among departments and agencies, to make sure those responsibilities are clearly understood, to monitor execution without attempting to control all its details, and to ensure cooperation and good communication among those responsible for carrying out the mission. Failure in these dimensions has been the root cause of the failure of intervention missions by the United States in general. Understanding the lessons learned from previous experiences is often left until moments of crisis, which is too late. The State and Defense Departments should be given joint responsibility for developing and maintaining the lessons-learned "library" of past experiences, for government-wide contingency planning for intervention, and for developing a program of education and training on this subject for the Cabinet and for department and agency staffs.

- **Maintain a superior but more efficient defense posture.**   The United States had a strong defense posture throughout the Cold War, although (unlike the Soviet Union) not at the cost of a strong economy. This effort was concentrated on

  - central strategic nuclear forces;
  - strong ground and air forces in Europe, and for reinforcing Europe, in conjunction with our NATO allies;
  - a strong military presence in Japan and Korea;
  - large naval forces, deployed in key areas and capable of worldwide deployment, both to assure control of the sea and to influence regional events;
  - massive airlift and sealift capability for global reach;
  - military bases around the world;
  - superior military technology for its forces;
  - a strong industrial and R&D base;
  - superior training; and

- strong security assistance programs for those allies that needed it and those countries threatened by the Soviet Union or by Soviet-supported countries.

The American people clearly support a continued strong defense effort. Obviously, that defense effort should not be at the high level of the Cold War, and indeed it is not. The defense budget has declined significantly in real terms since its 1985 peak of $387 billion (expressed in 1996 dollars, to eliminate the effects of inflation and to allow comparison; in 1985 dollars, the FY 1985 budget was $276 billion) to its anticipated 1996 level of $247 billion. The United States was devoting over 10 percent of GDP to defense in 1960, more than 6 percent in 1985, and will be spending slightly more than 3 percent in 1997. It is uncertain how much, if at all, defense spending will decline in subsequent years. Defense Secretary William Perry states that the defense budget has nearly bottomed out. But the pressures for continuing reductions in the absence of a more specific threat are likely to persist as long as achieving a balanced budget remains a goal of Congress and the executive branch. In any case, difficult choices and clearer priorities will be needed in order to achieve the most effectual balance among the armed forces.

In accordance with the security interests set out above, we should give priority in defense planning to the following:

1. Maintaining a strategic nuclear balance with Russia as long as that is necessary. Nuclear forces of this capability are likely to be large enough to deter any small nuclear power, even if such a power develops intercontinental ballistic missiles. To the extent feasible and cost-effective, however, we should deploy ballistic missile defenses as any serious missile threats develop; and to this end, we should pursue an R&D program that would allow such deployments early in the next century. Priority for missile defense should be given to theater ballistic missile defense because theater ballistic missiles are the greater near-term threat.

2. Maintaining expeditionary, mobile, deployable forces to help deter or otherwise cope with rogue states threatening to destabilize the international system and with complex humanitarian emergencies such as occurred in Bosnia, Somalia, and Haiti; and to make it unnecessary for any other country, fearing for its security, to mount a major new defense effort, thus precipitating a new arms race. Our military forces should be prepared to intervene in support of humanitarian emergencies in imploding countries, to intervene to prevent regional threats from succeeding, to intervene against hostile countries pursuing weapons of mass destruction, and to enforce embargoes of hostile states.

3. Maintaining an appropriate level of forward military presence that, although reduced from the Cold War period in Europe, is sufficient to help maintain U.S. leadership in key areas of the world, to help deter potential foes, and to buttress U.S. diplomacy. Korea, Japan, and some NATO countries welcome standing U.S. forces on their territory, but most countries do not. Instead, many countries welcome an offshore American naval presence, with its opportunities for periodic ship visits, naval exercises with local armed forces, and other forms of naval cooperation. Some countries will welcome occasional military-to-military exercises and other forms of cooperation with U.S. ground and air units. These forms of military presence contribute to building security relationships with friendly governments and to deterring regional threats.

4. **Assuring an appropriate level of readiness of our armed forces**, the highest level of readiness for our nuclear, forward-deployed, and naval and expeditionary forces, with lower levels of readiness for units expected to have sufficient warning time to prepare for later deployment.

5. **Balancing defense investments appropriately** among the size of armed forces to be maintained, the readiness levels of those forces, the need to maintain technological superiority (modernization) of the forces, and adequate sustainability of the forces in the new world circumstances. The latter requires a sufficient level of investment in modernizing the armed forces to discourage other countries from striving for technological superiority themselves, and to enable U.S. forces to succeed in future combat with as low a risk and as few casualties as is feasible. In particular, a relatively high level of R&D investment is needed to ensure technological superiority indefinitely.

6. **Increasing the operational efficiency and reducing the cost of the defense support establishment** by continuing to reduce the number of no-longer-needed military bases and by developing a long-term plan to acquire commercial-like services from private industry through competition wherever possible. The legislation that created a process to identify and dispose of unneeded military facilities has expired; it ought to be renewed, so that the costs of the defense base structure can be reduced in line with foreseeable military needs. Similarly, to reduce other support costs, a recommendation of the recent Roles and Missions Commission—namely, that commercial-like work commonly found in the general economy, such as maintenance and supply and fire protection, and similar activities, should be obtained through competition from the private sector wherever possible rather than by maintaining government facilities staffed by government civilian and military personnel—should be adopted, and a long-term plan developed to achieve maximum efficiency in meeting DOD's long-term support needs.

In sum, the international security interests of the United States will depend in the future, no less than in the past, on a continuing willingness of the American president and Congress to provide leadership on security matters. For the past half century, U.S. leadership on security matters has been constant and largely bipartisan. Those who, distracted by the decibel level of American democracy, believe that Americans lack the stamina to lead are not taking this historical record into account. The challenge now is to provide similarly consistent leadership in new circumstances and to ensure that our investment in the armed forces is sufficient to buttress our political leadership in the more turbulent and interdependent world of the twenty-first century.

Appendix F

U.S. International Economic Interests

Working Group on International Economics

Ernest Preeg, *chair**
Carter Beese
Judith Bello
Penelope Hartland-Thunberg
Erik Peterson
Sidney Weintraub
John Yochelson

* *principal author*

U.S. International Economic Interests

U.S. international economic interests are increasingly important, in both absolute and relative terms, in the post–Cold War "New World Order." Indeed, in the short to medium term, maintenance of an open-market international economic system has become one of only a few truly vital interests within the dictionary definition of vital as "essential to the continuance of life or full physical vigor." U.S. economic interests, moreover, need to be addressed in an integrated fashion, through a truly global strategy of international trade, investment, finance, and domestic economic policies. This contrasts with issues of a political/security nature, which, after a half century of Cold War global strategizing, have largely fragmented into local or regional conflicts, mostly of peripheral interest to the United States. Finally, economic issues are becoming more political and thus more central to overall international interests. National sovereignty is progressively constrained as a practical matter by a deepening network of economic policy commitments, trade dependencies, and large volumes of private capital flows. A specific example of the growing strategic importance of economic relationships is the integration of the Visegrad countries—the Czech Republic, Hungary, Poland, and Slovakia—into the Western grouping of industrialized democracies, wherein membership in the European Union (EU) would provide a bulwark against future Russian security threats comparable, although of a different character, to that of NATO membership.

This general statement of the primacy of U.S. economic interests is elaborated in the following sections in terms of the changing structure of the global economy, the current international economic system, and a prioritized policy agenda for pursuing short- to medium-term U.S. interests. The concluding section relates the economic policy agenda to longer-term objectives for the post–Cold War world order. First, however, it is useful to define the basic terms of reference with respect to (1) New World Order, and (2) U.S. economic interests in broadest terms.

- **New World Order:** This much-abused term is highly relevant if properly defined in terms of changed global relationships that evolved during the decade of the 1980s. Two fundamental changes took place. The first was the collapse of Soviet communism and the end of the East-West bloc-to-bloc orientation of U.S. strategic interests. U.S. security interests, as a consequence, have become far more regionalized, with less direct threat to the United States except for the nuclear proliferation issue. The second change was the blossoming of an unprecedented wave of technological innovation on a global scale that is still only at the early stages of adaptation. This second change has wide-ranging impact on the global economic system and is the point of departure for the following sections of this paper. The two changes together have produced a very different order of U.S. international interests, more heavily oriented toward political/economic issues, in both substantive and systemic terms.

- **U.S. economic interests in broadest terms:**   This is an elusive definition because almost all aspects of economic well-being, at the national and international levels, are interrelated, which can lead to lengthy and not very useful generalizations. For the purpose of this paper, which is to develop a specific set of policy objectives in the international economic field, the broad definition of U.S. economic interests can be stated briefly in terms of three basic goals:

1. **Sustained economic growth in the U.S. economy.**   The underlying measure of this goal is growth in national productivity. Sustained growth can provide both an improved level of economic well-being for the American people and the resources needed for defense and other global interests. There are many qualifying factors as to the path for achieving such growth, including social objectives and policies affecting the distribution of wealth, but the broad statement of objective is sufficient for the ensuing analysis of international economic issues.

2. **Sustained growth in other friendly nations.**   Prosperity in friendly nations not only contributes to U.S. economic performance through trade, but helps ensure a more stable and cooperative international security order as well. In this context, the causal relationships between open trade, economic growth, and democratization, discussed in the final section of this paper, are central to New World Order systemic thinking. Another benefit of prosperity in friendly nations is the enhanced capability for financial burden-sharing to achieve common objectives. The key linkage between these benefits is that they are mutually reinforcing through a very large "positive sum game" based on accelerating "gains from trade."

3. **Denial of economic well-being in adversary or renegade states.**   This is a more controversial area whereby actions are taken in the international economic field, such as trade embargoes or financial sanctions, to coerce such nations to change their policies or even their governments. In contrast with the mutually reinforcing relationship between goals one and two, the interaction of all three goals constitutes an actual or threatened "negative sum game," more in line with Cold War and earlier *Realpolitik* strategizing. Punitive economic measures, moreover, have a poor record of achieving their political objectives, and are subject to particular scrutiny in the policy framework section below.

☆ THE CHANGING STRUCTURE OF THE GLOBAL ECONOMY

The structure of the global economy changed fundamentally during the 1980s and continues to evolve rapidly in the 1990s. The directions of change are toward more open (i.e., trade dependent) national economies, a broadening scope of international transactions by sector and region, and growing net benefits, or gains from trade and investment, for almost all nations. Three central characteristics of this

Table 1
Growth in the Volume of World Merchandise Exports and Output,
1983–1995
(percentage change)
(1982=100)

	Exports	Output
1983	2.5	2.9
1984	8.5	4.8
1985	3.5	3.6
1986	4.5	3.5
1987	5.5	2.2
1988	8.5	5.5
1989	7.0	4.2
1990	4.9	0.0
1991	3.1	-1.0
1992	4.0	-1.0
1993	2.9	0.0
1994	9.5	3.5
1995	8.0	3.0
Cumulative	**101.6**	**35.7**

Sources: World Trade Organization, *International Trade: 1995 Trends and Statistics* (Geneva: WTO, 1995); World Trade Organization, WTO Press Release PRESS/144 (Geneva: WTO, March 22, 1996).

change are referred to here as "international trade writ large," "globalization of markets," and "industrial tripolarization."

- **International trade writ large** refers to the broadening scope of international transactions beyond trade in goods to trade in services, international investment, technology transfer in various forms, and the migration of professional as well as unskilled labor. These other areas of international transactions have always existed, but they are now of far greater relative importance, and tend to drive the overall trading system "writ large." The growth in trade is almost all in manufactured goods and services, which together accounted for 80 percent of total trade in 1994, and which are more closely integrated with international investment and technology transfer. Private sectors are at the forefront of this broadening process, creating pressures on governments for a corresponding broadening of the international economic policy framework. The policy areas of growing importance, moreover, such as foreign investment, technology development, financial services, and migration, are more sensitive politically at the national level.

- **Globalization of markets** is a consequence of the broadening scope of international transactions whereby national economies—and national firms—become

Figure 1
Indexes of World Output, Exports, and Investment, 1975–1993
(value in current U.S. dollars)

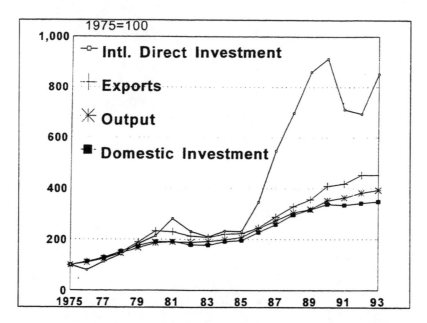

Sources: World Bank, internal figures; International Monetary Fund, *Direction of World Trade Statistics* (Washington, D.C.: IMF, June 1994).

more dependent on external markets. The volume of trade in goods has grown twice as fast as has national income since 1983 (as shown in table 1), and international direct investment has been growing even faster than trade (as shown in figure 1). The Uruguay Round agreement is projected to stimulate a net increase in trade of about 25 percent or more above this trend. Private capital markets have become highly integrated and, supported by new telecommunications technology, generate over one trillion dollars a day of mostly short-term international capital flows. The deepening dependence of economies on trade provides very large gains in income, particularly for smaller and "newly industrialized" countries, while at the same time limiting the power of governments to exert sovereign control over economic performance at the national level. The process of globalization is truly global in scope, but remains uneven by country, region, and sector.

• **Industrial tripolarization** is the most striking consequence of uneven globalization whereby international trade and investment have become increasingly concentrated within and among the three industrialized regions of Western Europe, North America, and East Asia. As shown in table 2, the total share of global imports of goods within the three regions increased from 40 percent in 1980 to 50 percent in 1993, while the corresponding share of trade among the three regions rose from 19 percent to 26 percent. As a consequence, trade among and with all other parts of the world, including South Asia, South America, Africa, the Middle East, and the former Soviet Union, dropped from 41 percent in 1980 to only 24 percent in 1990.

Table 2
Tripolarization of World Trade:
Western Europe, North America, and East Asia, 1980–1993
(percentage of world imports of goods)

	1980	1990	1993
Within the Three Poles	**40.0**	**49.2**	**49.7**
Western Europe	28.0	33.2	31.0
North America	5.9	6.5	7.5
East Asia	6.1	9.5	11.2
Among the Three Poles	**19.4**	**26.5**	**25.8**
Western Europe-North America	7.7	8.0	7.2
East Asia-North America	7.1	10.5	11.1
Western Europe-East Asia	4.6	8.0	7.5
All Other	**40.6**	**24.3**	**24.5**

Sources: International Monetary Fund, *Direction of Trade Statistics Yearbook* (Washington, D.C.: IMF, 1981, 1991, June 1994); *Foreign Trade Development of the Republic of China* (Taiwan: Board of Foreign Trade, 1994).

Note: **Western Europe** is defined as OECD Europe. **East Asia** is defined as Japan, South Korea, People's Republic of China, Hong Kong, Taiwan, and ASEAN (Brunei, Indonesia, Malaysia, Philippines, Singapore, Thailand). The same definitions apply to subsequent tables.

The shares of international investment and technology transfer emanating from the three industrialized regions are even higher, well above 90 percent, and the course of the world economy, including the growth effects of new technology applications, is dominated by these three regions.

This overall process of structural change in the world economy will continue unless there is a sharp reversal of the accommodating liberal trade policies of recent decades, which also accelerated during the 1980s and early 1990s. The recent accelerated trade liberalization included the Uruguay Round agreement, the North American Free Trade Agreement (NAFTA), the broadening and deepening of the European Union, and wide-ranging unilateral trade liberalization in developing and former Communist countries.

Three key conclusions about the changing world economy have particular relevance to the following discussion of the international economic system:

1. **The largely technology-driven restructuring of the world economy currently under way involves unprecedented gains from trade,** not only from the "static" effects of lower import prices from a reduction in trade barriers, but from the far more important "dynamic" effects of lower cost production, accelerated new technology adaptation, and the creation of new industries. The GATT secretariat estimated annual static gains from the Uruguay Round agreement of $184 billion (somewhat less than one percent of global output), but this estimate rises to $510 billion when some dynamic effects are included, and the figure would rise still higher if all dynamic effects were added. Economists have difficulty measuring the

full dynamic gains from trade, but those gains are increasingly evident to private and public sector leaders.

2. **Private sectors are almost always out in front of governments in the process of market globalization.**   Private-sector initiative in the Uruguay Round, for example, triggered the "zero-for-zero" approach to duty elimination by sector, with the result that the duty free share of nonagricultural imports in industrialized countries will rise from 20 percent to 44 percent. Recently adopted objectives for Asia-Pacific free trade by 2010–2020, for Western Hemisphere free trade by 2005, and for negotiation of a multilateral agreement on investment within the Organization for Economic Cooperation and Development (OECD) were likewise stimulated by private-sector pressures on governments.

3. **Technology-driven structural change at the national and international levels requires constant adaptation of the labor force,** which causes difficult adjustment for some workers and job anxiety for many. In the United States, only a very small share of this adjustment is caused by the trading sector, although protectionist demagogues try to blame almost all adjustment problems on imports. Such demagoguery was most evident in the 1993 NAFTA debate, although a year and a half later U.S. trade with Mexico, despite the peso crisis, has grown substantially in both directions, with relatively little adverse impact on U.S. jobs.

☆ THE INTERNATIONAL ECONOMIC SYSTEM

• **A three track trading system.**   The international trading system also underwent fundamental change during the 1980s. The liberal trading system broadened in scope, in keeping with the realities of international trade "writ large," and in geographic scope to include greater participation by developing and former Communist countries. It was also restructured from a predominantly multilateral system based on nondiscrimination (or most-favored-nation treatment) to a more balanced three track construct of multilateral commitments, comprehensive regional free trade agreements, and selective bilateral accords. This three track system continues to evolve in the 1990s, with particularly important interaction between the multilateral and regional tracks:

The multilateral track.   The GATT Uruguay Round agreement reduced trade barriers, broadened the multilateral system to include trade in services and intellectual property rights, and brought the troubled agricultural and textile sectors within the system of GATT rules. Developing countries, for the first time, undertook a broad scope of commitments, while the new World Trade Organization (WTO) strengthened the institutional basis for trade, particularly through the revised dispute settlement mechanism. Looking ahead, the multilateral agenda for the remainder of the decade is already taking shape and includes new issues such as competition and investment policies, the trade/environmental relationship, and labor standards, as well as plans for further trade liberalization.

The regional track.   Regional free trade is evolving in an even more dynamic way, and more than half of trade will likely occur within such agreements by the year 2000 or shortly thereafter. The EU is expanding to the east and NAFTA to the south, while the Asia-Pacific nations plan free trade by 2020. The subregional groupings of Australia/New Zealand, Association of Southeast Asian Nations (ASEAN), and MERCOSUR (Common Market of the South) are also significant. The EU and NAFTA, in particular, are "comprehensive" in that they go beyond the scope of policy covered by the multilateral WTO and include such areas as investment, transportation, financial services, and environmental policies. One result of recent U.S. regional initiatives in the Americas and with East Asia is that the North Atlantic relationship, long the backbone of U.S. trade and foreign policies, is the only major trade relationship not the subject of free trade deliberations, which has elicited interest in a transatlantic free trade agreement (TAFTA).

The bilateral track.   Selective bilateral accords also proliferated during the 1980s, largely as a result of U.S. Section 301 initiatives and an almost continuous process of structured U.S.-Japan bilateral negotiations. The U.S.-China trade relationship has also had an important bilateral dimension in view of the lopsided four to one trade imbalance favoring China and China's nonmembership in the GATT/ WTO. The outlook for the bilateral track is least clear among the three tracks. The Uruguay Round agreement should reduce existing bilateral quota arrangements, but other areas of trade and trade-related policies will still be subject to bilateral negotiations. U.S. trade policy initiatives toward Japan and China—involving what will be three of the four largest trading nations by early in the next century—will likely remain the most prominent components of the bilateral track, as witnessed in early 1995 by the intellectual property rights (IPR) dispute with China and the automotive sector dispute with Japan.

- **The international financial system.**   In contrast with the three track trade and investment policy relationship, which is becoming more structured and important in systemic terms, the official international financial system has receded dramatically in relative importance over the past two decades. International trade and investment are generally well accommodated by financing mechanisms, but they are predominantly private-sector oriented. Innovative "financial entrepreneurs" play key roles in organizing new investment projects, particularly in Asia. This acceleration of capital flows in the unofficial—or private—international financial system imposes new constraints on the extent to which governments can oversee and regulate economic activity within their territories. The capacities of central banks—even in key currency countries—to influence foreign exchange markets and financial flows are deteriorating. Governments are increasingly unable to respond to the volume and speed of cross-border flows.

The surge in private flows has similar implications for the International Monetary Fund (IMF) and the multilateral development banks (MDBs). Over time, the discipline imposed by market forces has replaced the conditionalities traditionally imposed by the IMF and the MDBs on developing countries. As a result, these institutions have been relegated principally to policing and financing the poorest and most troubled developing countries. Although such a function continues to be important, it affects a small share of international financial markets and reflects the progressive marginalization of the international financial institutions in the overall financial structure.

The Mexican peso crisis of early 1995 crystallized this evolving situation in international financial markets. The emergency financial support package helped stabilize the peso, but the principal conclusion drawn from this experience is that sound fiscal and noninflationary monetary policies at the national level are critical for maintaining exchange rate stability. Attempts to cover up unsound policies, as happened in Mexico, cannot be sustained for long before private markets respond with a vengeance. A more and more open trade and investment system, together with private financial markets integrated on a global scale, limit greatly the impact of official exchange rates and related financial policies. Steps to strengthen the international financial system, as proposed below, can have only a modest effect on this new central reality of international trade and finance.

☆ THE POLICY FRAMEWORK

The foregoing are the elements of a changed global economy encompassing world trade "writ large" and related changes in the international financial system. It is an evolving system that requires a forward-looking policy response to direct its future path, relating short- and medium-term objectives to longer-term systemic goals. For the trade and investment system, the operational imperative is to manage the three multilateral, regional, and bilateral tracks in a mutually reinforcing way toward more broadly defined goals, such as more open and balanced market access, more clearly established rules, and more equitable dispute settlement procedures. With respect to the international financial system, specific policy actions are less likely to affect overall trends. The operational imperative in this area should be to promote capital formation, reduce regulatory constraints, and encourage transparency.

The following are recommended short- to medium-term policy objectives to these ends, assessed in terms of being *vital, important,* or *beneficial* to U.S. interests. The concluding section of the paper relates this policy agenda to longer-term economic objectives and their relationship to the broader framework of U.S. global strategy in the post–Cold War order.

• **Strengthen domestic economic performance** (VITAL).   The benefits to the United States of an open international economic system can only be realized if economic policies at the national level act to stimulate adequate savings, investment, new technology development, improved education, worker training, and those other factors that will enable the country to stay at the forefront of the rapidly evolving and technology-driven new world economic order. At this juncture we must strengthen domestic economic performance not only to increase national productivity, but to avoid the negative reactions of global financial markets to inadequate policies. The specifics of such a national economic strategy are beyond the scope of this paper, but the objective is prominently presented as the number-one vital interest. At a minimum, such a strategy would include fiscal policies to eliminate the budget deficit and to revise the tax system so as to encourage higher levels of savings and investment. Also, such a strategy is feasible without resort to protectionist "industrial" policies that conflict with WTO commitments, and in fact such policies would generally be counterproductive to strengthening American economic performance.

- **Continue the process of broadening and strengthening the international trade and investment system, based on mutual access to markets in the United States and abroad** (VITAL).   This many-faceted central objective requires a detailed elaboration based on the changing structure of the world economy. The presentation here for trade policy is limited to noting priority objectives in terms of the three track policy structure:

1. **The consolidation and further broadening of the WTO multilateral trading system.**   Implementation of the Uruguay Round agreement is a first priority, particularly for commitments in the agricultural and textile sectors and for establishing the credibility of the greatly strengthened dispute settlement mechanism. Scheduled early inclusion in the WTO of financial and basic telecommunications services is likewise a priority goal provided for in the Uruguay Round agreement. The new WTO agenda should give high priority to bringing investment and related competition policies within the scope of the WTO so as to make it a world trade and investment organization, or WTIO. To this end, the May 1995 initiative in the OECD to negotiate a multilateral agreement on investment should be structured so as to be incorporated later into the WTO. The next stage of trade liberalization should include a major extension of zero-for-zero tariff elimination by sector, as pursued in the Uruguay Round, so as to eliminate tariffs on the large majority of non-agricultural trade.

The overlap between environmental objectives and trade policy, already established in the GATT/WTO, needs to be developed more fully, including severe restraint on or prohibition of unilateral import sanctions directed against the production standards in the exporting country. The need to bring labor standards within the trading system, in contrast, is not well established, and further review and consultation in this area are needed before attempting to add this controversial issue to the WTO action program. Finally, China and Russia should be supported in their interest in WTO membership, but the conditions for Chinese admission, in particular, should be tightly drawn in keeping with the strong international competitive position of Chinese industry.

2. **Further extension of comprehensive regional free trade agreements.**   Such agreements can and should be building blocks toward more open trade on a multilateral basis, and indeed should constitute the leading edge for the evolving global trading system. Regional free trade agreements have both "trade-creating" and "trade-diverting" effects, and they should be structured, in accordance with GATT criteria, to have predominantly trade-creating impact. Regional free trade can also

support political reform and democratization, as is the case in Europe and the Western Hemisphere. For the United States, extension of NAFTA to Chile and others in the Western Hemisphere is the first priority because hemispheric countries are already moving in this direction and are well disposed politically for early action. It is a historic opportunity to be seized.

The Asia-Pacific free trade objectives for 2010–2020, in contrast, are less clearly defined and raise a number of questions, particularly with respect to U.S.-Japan free trade by 2010 and U.S.-China free trade by 2020. Scheduled high level consultations to develop a "blueprint" for Asia-Pacific free trade should be based on a commitment to remain strictly in conformance with GATT Article XXIV, which is not fully the case in the 1994 report of the Eminent Persons Group.

Within Europe, early full membership in the EU of the Visegrad four should be strongly supported by the United States, not only for the political reason of bringing these countries into the Western industrialized grouping without adverse security implications for the former Soviet republics, but also because it should result in a substantial reduction of trade barriers by the Visegrad four vis-à-vis third countries, including the United States. These and any other free trade agreements by the EU, however, should again be carried out within a strict interpretation of GATT Article XXIV. For example, the initial free trade accords between the EU and the Visegrad four exclude agriculture and textiles, and this should not be accepted as in conformity with the GATT free trade requirement to include "substantially all of the trade" among members.

Finally, a transatlantic free trade initiative, based on the current administration's Transatlantic Agenda, should be supported in principle and developed as a priority objective. Such an agreement would be mutually beneficial in economic terms and would reaffirm the political cohesion of the North Atlantic grouping of industrialized democracies. An even more far-reaching objective to be explored is an open-ended OECD free trade agreement that would conveniently encompass the EU, NAFTA, and the more advanced East Asians (presumably the 2010 members of the APEC—Asia Pacific Economic Cooperation—free trade goal). Such a broadly-based free trade agreement—together with the OECD investment agreement—indeed holds the key to the eventual convergence of the multilateral and regional free trade tracks of the international trading system.

3. **A more targeted bilateral track.**   Bilateral trade objectives can be pursued usefully in new areas of policy not covered by the multilateral system—such as investment and competition policies—and to obtain more clearly defined U.S. trade relationships with Japan and China in terms of market access rules, with provision for complaint procedures and results monitoring. Examples are the agreements with Japan on public procurement contracts and with China on intellectual property rights. Numerical targets by sector, however, as was prominent during early Clinton administration policy toward Japan, are inimical to the multilateral trading system and should be avoided except in extreme circumstances where WTO commitments are absent or are being circumvented. In the latter case, the WTO dispute procedure should be fully utilized before unilateral sanctions are

considered. U.S. sanctions threatened against Japan in the automotive sector in the spring of 1995, in this regard, seriously undermined the new WTO and should not establish a pattern. China will remain predominantly a centrally-planned economy no matter how WTO participation is finally worked out, and the extraordinary, growing bilateral trade imbalance favoring China, even while China maintains a large trade deficit with other countries, is politically unsustainable in the United States. A high-level bilateral mechanism of broad scope should be established to develop a more satisfactory basis for trade.

- **Actively encourage a more stable and responsive international financial system** (VITAL).   While this is a vital U.S. interest, there is limited scope for policy actions to influence international financial markets. In light of the Mexican peso crisis, the IMF should be given a strengthened role for monitoring and ensuring transparency of national economic policies, so as to forestall or limit future currency crises, and a somewhat enhanced official capability for emergency financial packages may be warranted. At the same time, cross-border regulatory cooperation should be encouraged to ensure a coordinated response capability in times of financial crisis. Other policy actions should be directed toward lowering regulatory costs in private capital markets to reduce friction costs across borders, harmonizing standards in capital markets, and supporting capital market infrastructure in developing countries.

    The central policy consequence of recent experience, however, is the clearer realization that private financial flows can quickly overwhelm official intervention in financial markets in the absence of sound underlying policies at the national level. This implies that there is a more limited range of exchange-rate policy options between the extremes of monetary union and freely floating rates. Basic questions have also been raised and need to be assessed about the future role of the dollar as the predominant—and freely floating—key currency, as private transactions increasingly dominate currency markets.

- **Improve the effectiveness of foreign assistance programs in support of humanitarian needs, longer-term economic development, and democratization** (IMPORTANT-TO-BENEFICIAL).   U.S. economic assistance strategy, encompassing both bilateral and multilateral programs, needs a restructuring based on more clearly defined objectives and demonstrable results. Two areas of principal focus should be the transitional former Soviet bloc countries and the poorest, or "least developed" countries.

    Economic support for the transitional economies should be linked to the implementation of economic reforms for privatization, market-based pricing, fiscal balance, and trade liberalization. In this context, balance-of-payments or other indirect forms of "cash transfer" support to the government should be avoided because it can be counterproductive by providing both a cushion to postpone reforms and excessive financial power to central governments disposed to traditional authoritarian rule. Rather, project assistance targeted on particular bottlenecks to the reform process, and administered to the maximum extent through the private sector, should be the dominant form of support. In addition, unsafe nuclear power reactors in Russia and Ukraine constitute a specific important interest to the United States (and a vital interest to Western Europe), and deserve a larger support program than has been considered to date for a restructured energy sector.

Many of the least developed countries in Africa, Asia, and the Caribbean Basin (most prominently Haiti) have experienced a downward spiral of development which threatens tragic consequences internally, with important adverse effects on other countries. External adverse effects, moreover, are concentrated in neighboring countries, which makes the Caribbean Basin region of particularly important interest to the United States. Very large amounts of cash-transfer economic aid in recent years have achieved little success and can nurture a counterproductive relationship of chronic dependency on foreign aid, while strengthening the control of corrupt, authoritarian governments. "Nation-building" in political and economic terms is the challenge, which will require a more effective, longer-term commitment of external support. The development strategy should center on (1) project assistance to support private-sector job creation, (2) institution-building to strengthen the center of the political spectrum against destabilizing threats from the extreme left and right, and (3) the channeling of most to almost all economic aid through the private sector and nongovernmental organizations (NGOs).

The largest share of U.S. bilateral economic aid, almost half of the total, is provided in support of the Middle East peace process. However, because this assistance is predominantly for political objectives, it is not addressed here in economic terms.

- **Economic sanctions for foreign policy objectives** (BENEFICIAL).   Economic sanctions have a poor record of accomplishment, especially against repressive governments, and are often counterproductive by hurting poorer people and the business community within these countries while enabling the government to reap monopoly "contraband" profits. Haiti is a recent tragic example of a three-year embargo that devastated the economy and caused great suffering among the poor while still not accomplishing its purpose of restoring deposed President Aristide. (In the end, a U.S. military intervention was required). In addition, U.S. unilateral sanctions, such as used earlier against Vietnam and currently against Iran and Cuba, adversely affect U.S. commercial interests because other nations trade in and develop such markets at the expense of U.S. firms.

There is also a conflict in current U.S. economic sanction policy with respect to the question of whether normal commercial relations support or retard political and economic reforms in Communist and other state-dominated economies. For China and Vietnam, the current U.S. policy is that there is a positive effect from open trade, which appears to be correct, while for Cuba U.S. policy is the reverse.

A reassessment of U.S. policy is in order, with a view to reducing the use of economic sanctions for short-term foreign policy goals, particularly on a unilateral basis.

- **Maintain the long-standing U.S. leadership role in the international financial and economic system** (VITAL).   The growing importance of U.S. interests in the world economy and the dynamic complexities of the international trade and investment system at this historic juncture require strong leadership, both to take advantage of extraordinary opportunities and to avoid costly conflicts. For the short to medium term, at least over the coming five to ten years, the United States is uniquely able to play this leadership role because (1) it is at the forefront of new technology development and its international transmission, which is the driving force for the evolving international economic system; (2) it has a geographically diverse set of economic interests, principally in Europe, the Americas, and East Asia; and (3) it has a long-established capability and habit for exercising leadership. U.S. economic leadership has been based on enlightened economic and political self-interest that, in the post–Cold War setting, has become enhanced in commercial terms and, as described in the final section of this paper, refocused in political terms.

The U.S. international economic leadership role, over time, should be increasingly shared, particularly with the EU, Japan, and the next tier of industrialized and newly industrialized countries. This has been happening to some degree in various contexts in recent years—the "Quad" (the United States, the EU, Japan, and Canada) for trade, the G-5 (the United States, Germany, Japan, the United Kingdom, and France) for international finance, and the G-7 annual economic summit meetings in broadest terms. In particular, the EU played a stronger co-leadership role with the United States during the closing months of the Uruguay Round, and Japan exercises active leadership within APEC. Nevertheless, the EU remains regionally oriented within Europe while saddled with a cumbersome decision-making structure, and Japan is culturally reluctant to assert itself in multilateral forums and defensive about complaints concerning access to the Japanese market. Thus, for some years to come, the United States will have to remain the *primus inter pares* leader if there is to be strong leadership in the international economic field.

One critical dimension of continued U.S. leadership in world trade is the need for a more forceful and effective articulation of U.S. international economic interests to the American people. Structural changes under way in the national economy create anxiety in the work force, which predictably evokes a new high-tech Luddite reaction, resistant to change and attempting to blame adjustment problems at home on foreign trade. The near defeat of the NAFTA in 1993 was a result of such misleading protectionism, with no strong administration defense of the positive U.S. interests in NAFTA until the very end of the debate. The wide-ranging U.S. interests in a well-implemented open trade policy—writ large and in conjunction with the supportive national economic strategy noted in objective one above—must first be understood within the U.S. government, and then clearly communicated to the electorate.

☆ THE ECONOMIC-NATIONAL SECURITY INTERFACE

The foregoing is an international economic strategy for the next five to ten years centered on a continued strengthening of the international trade, investment, and financial systems. It would proceed in parallel with a national security strategy designed to confront local conflicts—from the Gulf War to Bosnia to Somalia to Haiti—and to prevent broader threats, including nuclear weapons proliferation. The architectonic question is how to fit the two together to form an overall post–Cold War global strategy.

The conclusion of this paper is that the broadening and deepening of the international economic system, if pursued with reasonable success, will play a more and more central role in such an overall world order, in both economic and political terms. The economic component was described earlier based on an economic system writ increasingly large, the globalization of national economies, and the growing gains from trade. The political component has two levels. Economic interdependence has direct political consequences through specified limits on national sovereignty, or at least on the ability to exercise such sovereignty. The deeper political significance of the rapid evolution of the international economic system since the mid-1980s—which goes to the core of the post–Cold War order—is the mutual reinforcement between economic liberalism and liberal democracy.

The long-term objective—or paradigm—for the international economic system, in fact, can be posed as the broadening of the grouping of industrialized democracies to the point where they constitute the large majority of world economic power, military capability, and population. The benefits of such a paradigm are that industrialized democracies are least likely to go to war with one another, have great incentives—through ever-increasing gains from trade—to resolve lesser conflicts in a cooperative manner, and have the financial resources to deal more effectively with the remaining troubled regions of the world.

The central role of the international economic system for pursuing this paradigm is based on two causal linkages. The first, well-established linkage is that a market-oriented liberal trade policy produces faster economic growth and thus the basis for broader industrialization and modernization. The second causal linkage is that such market-oriented growth is supportive of democratization. This is a more controversial linkage, especially if it is assumed to apply to all or almost all country situations. Even in its weakest form, however, that the forces for a decentralized and democratic political system grow as a national economy reaches the more advanced stages of industrial society—observation of the causal linkage is clearly evident. Only this weakest assumption is required for the paradigm outlined here.

The broadening of the industrialized grouping beyond the long-standing 24 members of the OECD to the point of including the majority of the global

Table 3
Cumulative Indicators for Projected Industrialized Democracies
(as a percentage of world total, 1991)

	Population	GDP	Exports	International Direct Investment
1. OECD (24)	16	77	71	96
2. OECD (30)[a]	19	80	75	96+
3. Line 2 plus other Western Hemisphere countries	25	84	79	96+
4. Line 3 plus Russia, Ukraine, Belarus, Baltic Republics	30	87	80	96+
5. Line 4 plus ASEAN	35	89	85	96+
6. Line 5 plus India	50	90	85	96+
7. Line 6 plus China	72	92	87	96+

Sources: Population data from *Statistical Abstract of the United States* (Washington, D.C.: U.S. Census Bureau, 1992) and *World Tables* (Washington, D.C.: World Bank, 1994). GDP data from *International Financial Statistics Yearbook* (Washington, D.C.: International Monetary Fund, 1994). Export data from *International Trade: Statistics* (Geneva: GATT, 1993). International direct investment data from *World Investment Report* (New York: United Nations, 1994).

[a] Line 1 plus Czech Republic, Hungary, Mexico, Poland, Slovakia, and South Korea.

population is, of course, a highly uncertain and longer-term prospect. Table 3 lists key tranches of additional country groupings. The first six additional countries—the Czech Republic, Hungary, Mexico, Poland, Slovakia, and South Korea—are reasonably well assured, and extension of the industrialized democracy grouping to the remainder of the Western Hemisphere and eastward in Europe to include Russia and the Ukraine are at least mutually agreed policy goals. It is the key Asian countries, however—the ASEAN countries, India, and China—that will be decisive, and the political outlook in this region is less clear.

This regional outlook for the broadening of the industrialized democracy grouping, incidentally, has a parallel in the regional track agenda for the trading system. The European and Western Hemisphere initiatives for regional free trade are firmly based on shared democratic political objectives, while the Asia-Pacific path to free trade, still only vaguely defined, carefully avoids reference to political underpinnings.

A critical dimension of the interface between the prospective scenario for the international economic system and the political-security conflicts that are plaguing the post–Cold War order is timing. Time is running in favor of a continued strengthening of the economic relationship, if managed properly, but clearly against the troubled political-security agenda. The United States is acknowledged to be the single unchallenged superpower in military terms today, but such a circumstance is only likely to prevail for another decade or two. Ever more transferable technologies increase the likelihood of proliferation of weapons of mass destruction, including use by terrorists, while highly unstable parts of the world threaten a broadening scope of internal violence with spillover external consequences. And China—the most likely rival to the United States as a global economic and military power over the long term—continues on a path of rapid technological advance and economic growth.

The post–Cold War global strategy for the United States is thus a dual arena construct, played out on largely separate playing fields, with critically distinct time frames:

- the WTO and regional free trade agreements, involving up to several decades for the evolving economic system, versus
- the UN Security Council and regional security arrangements, involving year-to-year violent conflicts in the regional pockets of political instability and failed economies.

It is not, however, a contrast between concrete short-term actions and nebulous, very long-term aspirations. The entire dual arena scenario will likely play out to a definitive resolution over the next decade or two or three, during the lifetime of the children and grandchildren of today's leadership.

This dual arena scenario, encompassing the interface between U.S. economic and national security interests, moreover, has various implications for priorities among foreign policy objectives, including resource allocation. For example, regional trouble spots far from home, including the Middle East, the Balkans, Central Asia, and sub-Saharan Africa, which have received inordinate attention and resources in the early 1990s, should be viewed as of somewhat less relative importance, while ASEAN countries, those of South Asia, and Latin America, largely ignored by U.S. foreign policy, should receive greater attention. China certainly looms even larger in importance, but with greater emphasis on its longer-term political/economic evolution than on immediate and limited foreign policy objectives.

The dual arena construct, finally, bridges the century-old dichotomy in the U.S. foreign policy debate between the thinking of Presidents Theodore Roosevelt and Woodrow Wilson, between balance-of-power alliances and multilateral covenants, between realism and idealism, between *Realpolitik* and cooperation. In fact, these dichotomies, while relevant to a certain extent in the past, are increasingly false and misleading distinctions today. There is a strong globalizing trend in the world economy, driven by a rate and degree of technological change never experienced before. There are wide-ranging threats to national and international security, although unrelated to major power relationships or alliances. The challenge for global strategy is to forge an amalgam of these extraordinary new realities so as to create a more prosperous, stable, and truly new world order.

Appendix G

Global Problems and Opportunities

Working Group on Global Problems and Opportunities

Jonathan Howe, *chair**

Brock Brower

Chester Crocker

Arnaud de Borchgrave

Max Kampelman

Joseph Montville

John Reinhardt

Andrew Schmookler

David Wendt*

* *principal authors*

Global Problems and Opportunities

With the end of the Cold War, the United States has exchanged one kind of insecurity for another. The insecurity of the nuclear peril and the bipolar confrontation with the Soviet Union has been exchanged for the unpredictability of a far more complex era. In this new post–Cold War world of global interdependence, financial markets, labor markets, fossil fuel emissions, ideas, technology, drugs, crime, and weapons—all know no boundaries. The United States is now part of an emerging global society. How we respond—and lead—in this new world of uncertainty and interdependence is the strategic issue at the turn of the millennium.

One thing is assured at the outset: the United States has no alternative to global leadership. Leadership by example, leadership through consultation, yes—but still, leadership. We can choose to retreat behind the facade of a defensive crouch—reacting to each new crisis as it occurs—or we can seek to help actively shape the forces that are now transforming the world. The latter course entails active leadership. It requires defining our priorities, marshaling our resources, and engaging others in identifying common problems and devising common solutions.

The problems discussed in this paper are among the most intractable and least likely to receive budget support during a time of severe financial constraints (a condition that seems likely to persist in the United States into the next century). At the same time, the end of the Cold War has created "opportunities" because, in the absence of great power rivalries, the window exists to begin countering these global threats by dealing with their root causes, rather than treating the symptoms as they occur.

Because of the premium placed on cooperative policy approaches, and because this family of issues does not represent immediate and direct threats to U.S. security, it contrasts with more traditional U.S. national security and foreign policy concerns. The latter, involving principally relations with other major powers, lend themselves much more readily to calculations involving the actual or potential use of force, undertaken with allies if possible but acting alone if necessary. But effective policy responses to both traditional interests and "global" concerns demand U.S. leadership. And, as we shall see, global issues also entail dangers that, while lying outside traditional foreign policy concerns, can pose threats to our national security.

Granted, the national security dimension of these challenges can be overstated. But there is a much greater danger in denying their existence altogether. A new mood in Congress and the American public seems determined to assert the primacy of American interests over global problems and opportunities, and to treat the latter increasingly as none of our concern.

This is short-sighted and self-defeating. The security, prosperity, and well-being of our own society can no longer be isolated from that of others. The challenge is to build on the structures that served us so well during the Cold War—NATO, the Conference on Security and Cooperation in Europe (CSCE, now the OSCE), the United Nations, our foreign aid program—adapting them to new challenges and modifying them in accordance with changed circumstances. There is nothing to be gained through a policy of systematically starving these institutions and programs of resources, denigrating their accomplishments, diluting and watering down their structures, circumventing their mechanisms and procedures, and generally going into a global pout.

☆ IMPORTANT U.S. INTERESTS

Interests in this paper do not easily fall under traditional definitions of national interests. Rather, these interests stand by themselves as shared interests of the peoples of the world. They are global interests in which Americans have a growing stake in a world that is increasingly interconnected. Nonetheless, while these challenges currently fall into the category of "important" or "beneficial" interests, a number of them could eventually escalate to the "vital" category if left unattended.

- **Combating the spread of syndicated and freelance crime.**   Adding to the crisis of control over our own borders is the increasing proliferation of lawlessness and global organized crime. Walls that came down with the defeat of communism have also, in many instances, removed barriers to the spread of syndicated and freelance crime, in the form of gangsterism, drug trafficking, money-laundering, narco-terrorism, trade-in-sex, smuggling of aliens, large-scale black marketeering and counterfeiting, and the proliferation of armed bands.

These are symptoms of a general breakdown of law and order within societies, which threatens to extend its reach even to places where the infrastructure of law enforcement is still intact. Indeed, the seemingly impenetrable cycle of drugs and violence in the United States cannot be divorced from the global criminal networks, which are well organized, flexible, and highly efficient. Global organized crime is crime without borders. National laws are now hopelessly out of date in countering this contagion. These trends threaten our sovereignty, our physical security, and our quality of life.

As terrorist and other extremist groups worldwide gain access to state-of-the-art portable weapons, powerful explosives, and chemical, biological, and even nuclear weapons, the consequences of not controlling these threats will grow. The recent truck bombing in Saudi Arabia, the bombing of the New York World Trade Center, and the chemical attacks on the Tokyo subway are graphic reminders of this growing danger.

- **Arresting the downward spiral of development that is taking place in parts of the Third World.**   The increased economic differentiation of the former Third World presents the United States with both opportunities and problems. Several administrations have stressed how much the United States stands to gain through growing markets in the newly industrialized countries (NICs) of Latin America and the Asia-Pacific region. At the same time, there is another category of former Third World countries—concentrated primarily in sub-Saharan Africa, South Asia, and the Caribbean—in which gross domestic product (GDP) has slipped steadily further behind population growth over the past decade and a half.

The elements of this "demographically driven downward spiral of development," as it has been termed by CSIS scholar Ernest Preeg, include poverty, population growth, and environmental degradation, all interacting negatively to compound one another. The case of Haiti illustrates this poverty/population/environment, or "multiple affliction," syndrome close to our shores.

Population growth and rapid urbanization in poor countries lead to densely settled, pathetically impoverished neighborhoods where, to take one measure of susceptibility to disease, an estimated 40 percent of the world's population lives without sanitary waste disposal systems or clean potable water. High-intensity regional wars create hundreds of thousands of refugees, devastate public health infrastructures, disrupt agriculture and diet, thrust economies into chaos, and ultimately render large populations susceptible to a variety of diseases.

The HIV virus causing AIDS, for example, has now infected more than 22 million people in the world, including 10 million in Africa alone. Recent projections suggest that by the year 2000, an estimated 100 million people may be infected, with much of this increase taking place in Asia, where the pandemic is now spreading most rapidly. Most of these HIV infections will end in premature death for young adults in their most productive years. Aside from the human costs, these figures will take a terrible economic toll: within families, with the loss of key breadwinners and the increased cost of care for the sick; and within whole societies, with the loss of productivity and the erosion of the human resource base.

And HIV/AIDS is but one of the many widespread diseases capable of massive societal disruption. Cholera, malaria, tuberculosis, and others remain as direct challenges to public health officials and societies at large. Our capacity to deal with these diseases will be a test of whether we can prepare ourselves to confront inevitable future threats to our public health.

But even where the previously listed threats are less immediate, the United States still has a stake in the amelioration of festering conditions of social pathology. Many of the places throughout the world that are suffering from these afflictions may be strategic backwaters, but the longer the world's wealthy "suburbs" ignore its deteriorating "slums," the more the slum dwellers themselves will be tempted to look for other neighborhoods. Paralleling these adverse economic and social trends are positive moves away from central planning and state economic control toward market-oriented economic reform and privatization. These trends have supplied the impetus for rapidly growing economies throughout large parts of Asia and Latin America, providing growing markets for U.S. exports and opportunities for U.S. investment.

But even in rapidly growing economies, the price for these gains has often been increased economic insecurity, unemployment, and income disparities. For countries in transition from centrally directed or state-controlled economies, these social costs of economic restructuring and "shock therapy" have, for the most part, not been equitably distributed. This contributes to some of the other adverse social and political trends noted below. It is also a concern for the United States because of the erosion of the social and political basis for continued economic reform.

- **Addressing problems associated with cross-border population movements.**
Widening economic disparities combined with large-scale civil disorder have also produced growing streams of people on the move. Many of these have flocked to our own shores. The U.S.-Mexican border is the longest border between an industrialized and a developing country in the world. Political unrest in Cuba and Haiti has produced thousands of boat people in recent years from these two countries. In Western Europe, too, increasing numbers of people arriving from North Africa, South and Southeast Asia, and Eastern Europe and the former Soviet Union in search of political asylum and/or economic opportunity have provoked an intense domestic political reaction against newcomers.

The domestic reaction in Europe and, increasingly, in the United States reflects a growing sense of loss of control of borders. In this sense, immigration is experienced in both settings as an issue of national security involving sovereignty. The other point of friction is unemployment and economic insecurity generally: others are perceived as taking "our" jobs. In fact, the net economic impact of immigrants is much more ambiguous. In many cases, immigrants either start new enterprises that actually create new jobs or occupy menial positions that would otherwise go unfilled.

Meanwhile, population displacements, which currently stand at about 50 million overall, are driven in significant measure by conditions of civil disorder. Better means of preempting or precluding these refugee flows at the source are needed to alleviate the strains placed on other countries.

- **Advancing human rights.**   It has long been widely accepted that all nations must recognize the importance of human rights and the responsibility of governments toward their people—the respect for human rights and fundamental freedoms, including freedom of thought, conscience, religion, or belief, without distinction as to race, sex, language, or religion. The promotion and effective exercise of civil, political, economic, social, cultural, and other rights and freedoms, all of which derive from the inherent dignity of the human person, are essential for free and full individual and societal development.

As noted in the international security section of this report (appendix E), the advancement of human rights is now an international as well as national matter.

There will always be a dividing line between "internal affairs," which are not to be interfered with by other states or by the UN, and the responsibility felt by the international community that it has a right and at times the duty to preserve peace and vital human values. In an era of increasing interdependence, however, an over-aggressive pursuit of a human rights agenda based solely on Western values could ultimately prove counterproductive, with respect to our ability to influence human rights in the first instance as well as to a range of other U.S. interests. This said, the United States, as a leading member of the United Nations and the world community in general, has a legal as well as a moral and practical interest in protecting and advancing human rights.

- **Reversing the problems of environmental degradation.**   As mentioned in the section on the "downward spiral of development" and in addressing the problem of rural to urban migration, abuse of the environment is a formidable and growing problem for the developing world. But the industrialized world also suffers similar challenges. Few industrialized countries have been willing to increase environmental expenditures substantially or to forgo economic growth to limit environmental dangers.

By the turn of the century, for example, there will be 21 "megacities" with populations of 10 million or more, including 18 in the developing world. To some extent, this trend reflects improved worldwide prospects for industrialization, which has historically coincided with the shift from a predominantly rural to urban population. But as previously indicated, increased rural-to-urban migration also frequently reflects a growing pressure of rural population on arable land, coinciding in many cases with deforestation, soil erosion, and other forms of environmental degradation.

Setting aside the domestic tug-of-war between developmental and environmental needs, a range of world environmental interests ultimately will affect our quality of life. Among many examples are improving the safety of nuclear power—preventing additional "Chernobyls," reducing the probabilities of oil pollution, stopping ocean dumping (toxic and nuclear), protecting against overfishing, minimizing acid rain, reducing ozone depletion, and alleviating global warming. Whether we like it or not, common international approaches are essential to finding equitable solutions to environmental issues. National boundaries will not protect us from the consequences of neglect.

- **Reconciling national interests with humanitarian intervention traditions.**   In terms of geopolitical consequence to the United States, humanitarian intervention is categorized as a "beneficial" interest. However, because these interventions are most often coupled with or related to "important" interests, distinctions are often difficult to make.

Where large-scale civil disorder and/or massive human rights violations warrant a more intrusive role by the international community, a growing body of global institutions and norms—the Helsinki accords, the Organization on Security and Cooperation in Europe, the UN Charter itself—now serves to legitimize intervention. Most recently, beginning with the first Iraq intervention sanctioned by UN Resolution 688, this has found expression in an emerging doctrine of "humanitarian intervention." This doctrine imposes implicit limits on the sovereignty of countries that fail to provide basic protection for their own citizens. Although international law recognizes the right of nations to form their own states—a choice that states are increasingly making in the face of pressures of ethnic fragmentation with the end of the Cold War—the international community has crossed the Rubicon with respect to interfering in the activities of individual nation-states.

In the post–Cold War world of ethnic tensions, intrastate conflicts, and proliferating civil disorder, these are no longer abstract issues of international law, but the concrete stakes of everyday political and even military relations between states. The resolution of these issues may also go beyond purely an assessment of interests. Conflicts over national self-determination touch basic issues of national identity. Similarly, issues of U.S. involvement in these conflicts—and in other global cataclysms involving human rights as well as humanitarian catastrophes—go to the heart of issues of our identity: what we stand for as a nation and what we mean to ourselves. They also go to the basic issue of whose problems these are in the first place. Global human rights, humanitarian, and human development issues are not necessarily only "somebody else's problem." Depending on how we define our identity, they touch us all.

☆ POLICY RECOMMENDATIONS

Each of the interests outlined above has a significant unilateral, regional, and international component. Effective policy responses at all three levels, however, require vocal and consistent U.S. leadership from the president on down. In the final analysis, whether America's focus is defined in broad or narrow terms regarding the full range of global problems and opportunities, it remains squarely in the U.S. interest to take the lead in tackling these issues and meeting shared concerns. Such leadership is urgently needed in a new era.

What follows is a series of policy recommendations for U.S. global leadership, designed to counter the adverse trends and concerns noted and to bring opportunities more within our reach. These strategies are to a large extent complementary, not mutually exclusive. Some of them address the root causes of violence and instability. Others are more concerned with controlling and managing the consequences of these conditions.

For the United States, the art of effective leadership will consist of devising a mix of approaches that makes the best use of our resources and leverages them most effectively in combination with others. The cost-effectiveness and feasibility of these approaches will be critical in determining our capacity to enlist the cooperation of others and to demonstrate that we mean business. Most of all, we need to make clear our commitment to finding shared solutions to shared problems, even if this means not getting all that we want.

- **Develop an integrated international capability for combating global organized crime and terrorism.**   When dealing with the issue of global organized crime—and in particular, with criminal groups themselves—the more traditional instruments of diplomacy are not applicable. The United States therefore must continue to negotiate with its key allies and friends to better attack this problem. Traditional links with our intelligence and law enforcement counterparts in other countries must be expanded, and there should be no delay in developing new links with non-traditional partners with whom we share this common interest. The ability to successfully uncover transnational organized terrorist cells and criminal enterprises, and to track and even to anticipate their moves, requires the utmost cooperation between agencies and governments. This, of course, can be achieved only with a high degree of support and commitment within our own government. Closer integration of law enforcement, military, intelligence, and diplomatic capabilities is needed to solve very complex political problems and to ensure better preparedness. U.S. readiness to counter and defend against terrorist threats involving the use of high explosives and weapons of mass destruction needs significant improvement.

- **Adopt trade and investment policies that facilitate job creation in impoverished countries.**   In economic terms this strategy requires U.S. trade and investment policies that will serve to create "jobs there" as an alternative to a constant stream of people seeking "jobs here." This reflects a basic dilemma confronted by many impoverished countries (Haiti is an example): either they will export their goods, or they will be forced to export their people.

Our own example can be a significant factor in the way we exert support for these tendencies. It is particularly important to maintain our own continued and strengthened commitment to principles of free trade. Prospects for political stability in the developing world depend on significant progress in job-creating economic growth. This, in turn, requires access to the markets of the United States and other industrialized countries. In some cases, expanded trade and investment in countries of emigration has been shown, in the short term, to lead to higher levels of economic mobility resulting in more outmigration, not less. But in the long term, pressures for outmigration begin to abate as a response to expanded economic opportunities. So, in the end, free trade produces a net benefit for all of those involved.

A strategy for keeping people in place is also key to combating urbanization. By enhancing opportunities and raising incomes in the countryside, strategies of rural economic development can, over the long term, provide incentives for people to remain on the land. These strategies can also alleviate pressures to immigrate to the United States because rural-to-urban migration is often the first link in a chain leading ultimately to migration overseas.

The immediate priority with regard to this transmigration is to keep things from getting worse. The situation in parts of Africa is particularly serious. With population growth rates outstripping rates of economic growth in many African countries, and with little immediate prospect of mobilizing the private investment flows that are propelling other parts of the world toward prosperity, this will be no easy task. Perhaps the best that can be done with limited available public resources is for the industrialized world to organize a kind of "holding action" for these regions until other countries can join in the international assistance effort.

In the interim, the second part of the answer is to work with such countries as those of Africa to develop their own capabilities. Africans must develop the political will and the institutional and human resource capacities to find African solutions to African problems. This begins with stanching the exodus from Africa of its own most talented leaders. By 1987 the number of higher-educated Africans migrating to the industrialized world had grown to 23,000 per year from its 1960–1975 level of 1,800. This outward flow of human resources must be arrested and reversed.

- **Gauge the pressure we apply on other countries in pressing for political and economic reform.**   The worldwide trend of economic liberalization and democratization must continue. This trend, which took root in Latin America in the 1980s, had by the end of the decade spread to Eastern Europe and the former Soviet Union, and is now transforming parts of Asia as well as Africa. However, a final caveat in supporting other countries' moves toward economic and political reform is that too much reform, too quickly, can be counterproductive. Unless the social costs of economic restructuring—such as unemployment and loss of subsidies—are borne equitably, structural adjustment can be a prescription for social and political unrest.

For this reason, at the same time that it is throwing its weight behind efforts at economic policy reform, the United States needs to continue or increase its traditional commitment in support of "basic human needs"—health, family planning, education, and other social services. The same is true of U.S. support for democratization. In ethnically divided countries, where a culture of pluralism has yet to take root, a premature push toward democratization may backfire. There are signs that this may have been one factor in the crisis in Rwanda.

Where countries are in transition from one-party rule and state-controlled economies, our policies in aid, trade, and investment can be important statements of political support for making the hard choices. We must nurture carefully the forces of political and economic reform—predicated on the knowledge that in the absence of policy reform, significant action on other issues of importance to the United States (e.g., population stabilization, environmental improvement, containing the spread of AIDS) will not be fruitful. We must also labor secure in the knowledge that, in the long run, the reform tendencies will win out.

- **Continue to press for human rights around the world and remain engaged with those countries whose policies in this area are inconsistent with our own.** The United States must clearly define a position on this issue that reconciles its geopolitical interests with its humanitarian traditions and principles of human rights, and its international responsibilities with its limited resources and reserves of public support. We must also be prepared to indicate those circumstances when we will not ignore atrocities such as genocide, man-made starvation, and ethnic cleansing and the mass population movements that they often invoke.

In addition to supporting developing countries in balancing difficult trade-offs between structural economic adjustment and social justice, or between political democratization and ethnic fragmentation, the United States needs to establish priorities relating to the movement of people. In political terms, the choice is between upholding our commitments under international law to refugee protection and support for human rights, and avoiding large and disruptive refugee flows resulting from human rights abuses and political repression.

Reconciling these two imperatives may require the international community to resort to more intrusive measures, including military intervention, to provide protection in place for victims of human rights abuses. Likewise, in situations where civil order has broken down completely, military intervention may be necessary to prevent atrocities.

- **Sustain, broaden, and intensify U.S. participation in multilateral and bilateral environmental protection initiatives.**   Beyond the difficult challenges of humanitarian intervention, Americans need to develop new attitudes toward shared world concerns. Whether dealing with the environment, overpopulation, or a host of other international issues, progress will depend heavily on American attitudes and willingness to lead in finding solutions. In the past, we have often shrunk from leadership on these issues, regarding some of the international mechanisms proposed for alleviating global problems as a threat to our sovereignty, our wealth, and our way of life. Rather than being overly defensive, we would better protect our future by actively leading in shaping solutions.

With regard to the environment, U.S. participation in multilateral, bilateral, and nongovernmental initiatives needs to be sustained, broadened, and intensified. If we simply fight a holding action in this area rather than actively promoting sensible policies, we will lose in the long run. In particular, the United States needs to be more attentive to the opportunities for "win-win" solutions through increased flows of American capital and technology to address environmental priorities in developing countries (e.g., water supply and treatment, waste management, and air pollution control). We also must become leaders in finding solutions to the environmental problems that threaten the long-term health of the environment in the developing world.

- **Develop a strong capability in preventive diplomacy.**   Obviously, the most cost-effective method of treatment is to prevent the disease in the first place. Investing in prevention is the ideal long-term strategy for U.S. global leadership. It mobilizes resources to address the roots of a problem, engages us and helps us build political capital at the outset with local leadership groups, and provides the greatest leverage in shaping the outcome in accordance with our interests. With its emphasis on consensus-building and the nurturing of long-term common interests, prevention is also the most appropriate strategy for pursuing our interests in a new era in which military force is only one—and less likely to be the most relevant—of the instruments of power and diplomacy.

This strategy puts a premium on effective early-warning and intelligence-gathering systems that may not produce immediate results. This can potentially tax the patience of the public because, like any investment, it demands discipline: paying now to avoid paying more later. Results are not always guaranteed, but an appeal to the American public must be made in credible cost-benefit terms that they can both understand and support.

- **Support confidence and security building measures.**   The United States must support confidence and security building measures (CSBMs) with other countries as an essential element of the preventive diplomacy component of its national security framework. These measures facilitate communication, reduce uncertainties, and promote cooperation by enhancing transparency, providing structures for identifying intentions pursuant to national interests, and establishing limits or defining boundaries of action. CSBMs may be implemented as unilateral, bilateral, or multilateral initiatives and have varying scopes of derivation, regional application, and enforcement potential—but all share the common goal of promoting peace and security.

The United States has long engaged in CSBM activity, dealing with a range of issues from territorial border recognition and multilateral communications networks, to exchanges of military data and activity monitoring mechanisms, to "no-first-use" pledges and agreements outlining how nations should interact during various contingencies. However, with an ever-increasing premium placed on preventing or averting conflict, now more than ever we must seek to maximize the utility of this valuable tool (in terms of both depth and frequency) across the full spectrum of international relations.

- **Support and strengthen those institutions that can mitigate and solve disputes.**   Clearly, leadership means working with our friends and allies; otherwise, it is no different than unilateral U.S. action. The challenge is to find a position between acting as global policeman and ignoring all crises. This entails developing a workable global division of labor. Recent experiences—from Somalia to the former Yugoslavia—have rendered the term "multilateral" synonymous with weakness and failure to many in America. This is shortsighted. America is neither capable nor willing to police the world. Strong, streamlined, and functioning multilateral institutions—from the UN on down—are required for the United States to promote mutual interests while sharing the burdens more equitably with our allies and friends. This is particularly the case when dealing with circumstances in which the shared U.S. and world interest is primarily humanitarian in nature.

One strategy that does not rely for its success on elimination of the sources of conflict and violence is a strategy of supporting and selectively strengthening those institutions that can buffer, contain, and resolve violent conflict. A key dimension of international effectiveness is the strength of governing institutions, measured by their legitimacy, efficacy, and solvency.

Former Assistant Secretary of State Chester Crocker, principal architect of the 1989 Namibia Accords, has noted that the problem of growing global lawlessness—the "global law and order deficit," as he calls it—can be traced to a fundamental deficit of norms, rules, and institutions by which nations seek to regulate international life. This deficit also extends to implementing and enforcement mechanisms, including a possible multinational military capability (e.g., a UN rapid deployment force) capable of enforcing an emerging consensus on standards of "humanitarian intervention."

Because of the need for flexible alternatives, it is in the interest of the United States to enhance the UN's credibility, not to discredit it further. The UN has some clear successes to its credit. In Cambodia, for example, it succeeded against all odds in helping a war-torn nation to restore and maintain peace, repatriate refugees, supervise elections, and rebuild. We need to build on these successes. In other cases, such as Somalia, it has been less successful. Here we need to learn from our mistakes: a principal lesson that emerges from Somalia, for example, is to avoid broadening the UN's mandate while simultaneously reducing its capabilities.

There may be some contingencies in which an international force of volunteers can provide a stopgap between narrow national interests and mutually shared world interests. Although such a force would raise questions of command, funding, and stationing of the troops, it would also be free of the conflicting calculations of national interest that plague current UN missions. The concept of a UN crisis-response civilian-military headquarters, augmented by trained volunteer units from member nations, would be a first step toward establishing a modest international capability for responding rapidly to humanitarian disasters such as genocide in Rwanda. The ideas being advanced by Canada, the Netherlands, and Denmark for a trained and ready on-call UN rapid-response force merit careful consideration. Significant internal reform will be needed, however, if the UN is to deal effectively with humanitarian catastrophes, failed states, and ethnic conflict.

The UN Secretariat needs to streamline its organization in order to provide more responsive and effective support to its field operations. The UN office for peacekeeping should be strengthened and given the authority to ensure the cooperation and responsiveness of other UN offices and agencies associated with peacekeeping.

Security Council resolutions need to be backed by adequate resources. In the area of peacekeeping, this may mean budgetary support of humanitarian, political, and civil efforts such as restoration of local police in addition to military resources.

To ensure its viability, efficiency, and effectiveness for the next century, the UN needs a total bottom-up review of all of its functions with a commitment to downsizing and more cost-effective use of its assets. Nonetheless, the future relevance and utility of the United Nations is clear. Therefore, the United States should set the example by paying off its arrears and should reward reform by beginning to pay its future obligations in the year payments are owed rather than a year later.[*]

In the realm of domestic politics, the challenge of institution-building runs the gamut, from economic and policy reforms to effect a transition from centrally planned economies and one-party states, to the rebuilding of "failed states" lacking an entire infrastructure of governance. The guiding principle of U.S. involvement across this spectrum of contingencies must be that the United States can only have lasting impact where nations are already committed to finding their own solutions.

Peacekeeping, for example, is an area where Africans seem increasingly inclined to solve their own problems. Beginning with a resolution adopted at the 1993 meeting of the Organization of African Unity (OAU) in Dakar to create a peace-keeping "mechanism" under OAU auspices, Africa has taken tentative steps toward making its own peacekeeping ability a reality. The U.S. Congress, through its 1994 African Peacekeeping Act, and the State Department have played important roles in quietly supporting this evolution. Even without significant peacekeeping capa-bilities of its own so far, the OAU can play a valuable role in giving us its own assessment of how we can help be part of the solution—their solution—on the political level. The United States' farsighted recognition of the promise of this incipient homegrown peacekeeping capability and expertise deserves continued and increased support.

Where national political leadership has made such a commitment, U.S. exper-tise and experience in such areas as developing legal infrastructures, reforming tax systems, securing property rights, and the like can make a significant difference. But this requires a matching commitment on the part of those receiving such assis-tance to making the hard choices demanded by reform. The proper role of multi-lateral involvement and development assistance is to help sharpen and build political capacity and support for these choices, not to let countries off the hook.

- **Align academia with today's interdependent world.**   Finally, steps should be taken to internationalize college curriculums, focusing on issues of global interde-pendence, foreign language proficiency, and cultural training.

☆ CONCLUSION

The above listing of issues might seem to imply that the new agenda of global prob-lems and opportunities is purely the product of a set of impersonal forces. If this

---

[*] Representative Lee Hamilton has called for the following specific UN reform measures:
- the UN regular budget should be frozen at current levels and then cut in selected areas including regional economic commissions, UNCTAD, global international conferences, and the UN Secretar-iat staff;
- the UN specialized agencies should be scaled back to perform only their core functions of standard-setting and information-gathering; and
- the UN offices for peacekeeping and the Inspector General should be strengthened.

were so, the old "functionalist" paradigm of world peace through collaboration outside the strictly political realm might suffice as a conceptual framework. But many of these issues are in fact deeply rooted in politics.

Mass famine, for example, almost never occurs in isolation from political factors, either as cause or as effect. At the very least, democratic institutions provide an essential set of feedbacks and incentives to hold policymakers accountable for failure to anticipate impending disaster. More darkly, starvation can be deliberately used as an instrument of political warfare.

In the same way, most of the ethnic conflicts that have broken out in the post–Cold War period have reflected the deliberate manipulation of ethnic animosities and insecurities by pseudo-democratic leaders for their own political purposes. In this sense, even the worldwide trend toward democratization can, in some circumstances, represent a cause for concern as well as an opportunity for the United States.

The most relevant question for the United States with each of the global trends and concerns identified is the extent to which the source of instability described is capable of being fused with a hostile intent so as to pose a threat to the United States and its interests. Where, in cases such as radical Islam, festering conditions of instability are capable of being imbued with a political or ideological dynamic, instability and anarchy can pose direct threats to U.S. interests. Elsewhere, anarchy may be disconcerting or morally troubling, but it is not necessarily a U.S. security concern.

Nonetheless, it will be difficult at times to draw the line between demonstrable national security interests and legitimate human concerns. Policymakers must be responsive to the level of public outrage, which may vary in relation to the crisis. But we must be realistic and realize that, in the case of intervention, although we may be able to stop the fighting, we cannot necessarily create a democracy. There must be a way to perform a cost-benefit analysis, comparing the amount of good that can be accomplished with the financial and human cost necessary to attain it. We must be prepared to pay a price, but not an excessive one. And we must also be prepared to consider the cost—to our values as well as our interests—of inaction.

The United States will have to learn to live with uncertainty. Situations beyond U.S. control are likely, at any given moment, to outnumber or outweigh situations in which U.S. influence or intervention can be decisive. In these circumstances, the task for a pragmatic U.S. policy that reflects fundamental ideals will be to identify the greatest threats to its values and interests and to marshal its resources and those of others where international action has the greatest chance of affecting the outcome. Elsewhere, the U.S. role will almost certainly be limited to working with others to organize holding actions until underlying conditions can improve.

Finally, we need to recognize that solutions to global problems require the cooperation of many nations. In many circumstances, the most important U.S. contribution will be as a catalyst and a leader by example in promoting world cooperation to meet the challenges posed by these critical issues.

About the Participants

Carter Beese, CSIS Senior Adviser; former Commissioner of the U.S. Securities and Exchange Commission.

Judith Bello, former General Counsel to the U.S. Trade Representative; former member of the Advisory Committee, Export-Import Bank.

Brock Brower, former CSIS Director of Public Affairs; former writer and producer, ABC News *20/20*.

Harold Brown, CSIS Counselor and Trustee; former Secretary of Defense.

Zbigniew Brzezinski, CSIS Counselor and Advisory Board Cochairman; former National Security Adviser.

Stanton Burnett, CSIS Senior Adviser and former Director of Studies; former Counselor and Director of Research, U.S. Information Agency.

Richard Burt, CSIS Senior Adviser; Codirector of the G-7 Council; former Assistant Secretary of State for European and Canadian Affairs; former U.S. Ambassador to the Federal Republic of Germany.

Keith Bush, CSIS Senior Associate in Russian and Eurasian Studies; former Director of Radio Liberty Research.

Andrew Carpendale, former Deputy Director of Policy Planning, U.S. Department of State.

William Clark, CSIS Senior Adviser on Asia; President of the Japan Society; former Assistant Secretary of State for East Asian and Pacific Affairs; former U.S. Ambassador to India.

Anthony Cordesman, CSIS Senior Fellow and Codirector of Middle East Studies; former National Security Assistant to Senator John McCain; former Director of Policy, Programming, and Analysis, U.S. Department of Energy.

Chester Crocker, Chairman of the U.S. Institute of Peace; former Assistant Secretary of State for African Affairs.

Arnaud de Borchgrave, CSIS Senior Adviser; former Editor in Chief of the *Washington Times;* former Senior Editor and Chief Correspondent at *Newsweek* magazine.

Paula Dobriansky, former Director of European and Soviet Affairs, National Security Council.

Richard Fairbanks, CSIS Managing Director of Domestic and International Issues; former U.S. Ambassador-at-Large; former chief negotiator for the Middle East peace process.

Banning Garrett, CSIS Senior Associate in Asian Studies.

James Goldgeier, Professor of Political Science, The George Washington University.

Gerrit Gong, holder of the CSIS Freeman Chair in China Studies and Director of the CSIS Asian Studies Program; former Special Assistant to the Under Secretary of State for Political Affairs.

Stephen Hadley, former Assistant Secretary of Defense for International Security Policy.

Lee Hamilton, Ranking Democratic Member, Committee on International Relations, and former Chairman, Committee on Foreign Affairs, U.S. House of Representatives.

Penelope Hartland-Thunberg, CSIS Senior Associate for Economic and Business Policy; former member of the U.S. Tariff Commission.

ADM Jonathan Howe, USN (Ret.), Executive Director of the Arthur Vining Davis Foundation; former UN envoy to Somalia; former Deputy National Security Adviser.

Fred Ilké, CSIS Distinguished Scholar; former Under Secretary of Defense for Policy; former Director, U.S. Arms Control and Disarmament Agency.

Douglas Johnston, CSIS Executive Vice President; founder and former Director, Harvard University Executive Program in National and International Security.

Max Kampelman, CSIS Senior Adviser and Advisory Board member; Vice Chairman of the U.S. Institute of Peace; former Counselor, U.S. Department of State; former Ambassador and Head of the U.S. delegation to the Negotiations on Nuclear and Space Arms.

Walter Laqueur, holder of the CSIS Henry A. Kissinger Chair in National Security Policy; Chairman of the Board of Editors of the *Washington Quarterly*; former Director of the Institute of Contemporary History in London.

Richard Lugar, Chairman of the Subcommittee on European Affairs and former Chairman, Committee on Foreign Relations, U.S. Senate.

Edward Luttwak, CSIS Senior Fellow in Preventive Diplomacy; former holder of the CSIS Arleigh A. Burke Chair in Strategy.

Dave McCurdy, former Chairman, Permanent Select Committee on Intelligence, and Member, Committee on Armed Services, U.S. House of Representatives.

Joseph Montville, Director of the CSIS Program in Preventive Diplomacy; founder and former Director of the Office of Global Issues, Bureau of Intelligence and Research, U.S. Department of State.

Robert Murray, President of the CNA Corporation; former Director of National Security Programs, Harvard University; former Under Secretary of the Navy.

Ken Myers, Legislative Assistant for National Security Affairs, Office of Senator Lugar.

Tom Navratil, Foreign Service Officer, U.S. Embassy in Moscow, Department of State; former International Affairs Fellow, Council on Foreign Relations.

Robert Neumann, CSIS Senior Adviser; former U.S. Ambassador to Saudi Arabia, Afghanistan, and Morocco.

LTG William Odom, USA (Ret.), Director of National Security Studies, Hudson Institute; former Director of the National Security Agency.

Erik Peterson, CSIS Vice President and Director of Studies; former Director of

Research for Kissinger Associates.

Ernest Preeg, holder of the CSIS William M. Scholl Chair in International Business; former U.S. Ambassador to Haiti; former Chief Economist, U.S. Agency for International Development.

John Reinhardt, former Director of the U.S. Information Agency; former U.S. Ambassador to Nigeria.

John Richards, Executive Assistant to the Executive Vice President, CSIS.

Brad Roberts, Institute for Defense Analyses; former CSIS Fellow in International Security Studies and Editor of the *Washington Quarterly*.

Peter Rodman, Director of the National Security Program, Nixon Center for Peace and Freedom; Senior Editor of *National Review*; former Deputy Assistant to the President for National Security Affairs.

John Rogers, CSIS Adjunct Fellow; former Deputy Assistant Secretary of Defense for Plans and Operations.

Andrew Schmookler, independent writer and lecturer.

Simon Serfaty, CSIS Director of European Studies; former Director of the John Hopkins Foreign Policy Institute.

Anthony Smith, CSIS Executive Vice President and Chief Operating Officer; former Principal Military Deputy for NATO and Europe, Office of the Secretary of Defense.

Don Snider, holder of the Olin Chair in National Security Studies, U.S. Military Academy; former Director of the CSIS Political-Military Studies Program.

Stephen Solarz, CSIS Senior Adviser; former Chairman of the Subcommittee on Asia and the Pacific, Committee on Foreign Affairs, U.S. House of Representatives.

Richard Solomon, President of the U.S. Institute of Peace; former Assistant Secretary of State for East Asian and Pacific Affairs; former U.S. Ambassador to the Philippines.

Michael Van Dusen, Minority Chief of Staff, Committee on International Relations, U.S. House of Representatives.

Sidney Weintraub, holder of the CSIS William E. Simon Chair in Political Economy; former Deputy Assistant Secretary of State for International Finance and Development; former Assistant Administrator of the U.S. Agency for International Development.

David Wendt, Dean of the CSIS Intern Scholars Program; former Director of the CSIS International Economic and Social Development Program.

John Yochelson, President of the Council on Competitiveness; member of the Advisory Committee on Investment, U.S. Department of State; former CSIS Vice President for International Business and Economics.

Dov Zakheim, CSIS Senior Associate in Political-Military Studies; former Deputy Under Secretary of Defense for Planning and Resources.

Robert Zoellick, CSIS Senior Associate; former Under Secretary of State for Economic and Agricultural Affairs; former Counselor, U.S. Department of State.